DATE DUE

Demco, Inc. 38-293

Listening to
Battered Women

Psychology of Women

BOOK SERIES

Listening to

Battered Women

A Survivor-Centered Approach to Advocacy, Mental Health, and Justice

LISA A. GOODMAN AND **DEBORAH EPSTEIN**

Foreword by Judith L. Herman

American Psychological Association
Washington, DC

Published by
American Psychological Association
750 First Street, NE
Washington, DC 20002
www.apa.org

To order
APA Order Department
P.O. Box 92984
Washington, DC 20090-2984
Tel: (800) 374-2721
Direct: (202) 336-5510
Fax: (202) 336-5502
TDD/TTY: (202) 336-6123
Online: www.apa.org/books/
E-mail: order@apa.org

In the U.K., Europe, Africa, and the
Middle East, copies may be ordered from
American Psychological Association
3 Henrietta Street
Covent Garden, London
WC2E 8LU England

Typeset in Minion by Circle Graphics, Columbia, MD

Printer: Maple-Vail Book Manufacturing Group, Binghamton, NY
Cover Designer: Naylor Design, Washington, DC
Technical/Production Editor: Harriet Kaplan

The opinions and statements published are the responsibility of the authors, and such opinions and statements do not necessarily represent the policies of the American Psychological Association.

Library of Congress Cataloging-in-Publication Data

Listening to battered women : a survivor-centered approach to advocacy, mental health, and justice / by Lisa A. Goodman and Deborah Epstein. — 1st ed.
    p. ; cm. — (Psychology of women book series)
 Includes bibliographical references and index.
 ISBN-13: 978-1-4338-0239-3
 ISBN-10: 1-4338-0239-2
 1. Abused women—Services for. I. Goodman, Lisa A. II. Epstein, Deborah, 1962-
III. American Psychological Association. IV. Series.
 [DNLM: 1. Battered Women. 2. Domestic Violence—prevention & control.
3. Feminism. 4. Mental Health Services. 5. Social Control, Formal. 6. Socioeconomic
Factors. WA 309 L773 2008]

 HV1444.L57 2008
 362.82'92—dc22
                                2007016646

British Library Cataloguing-in-Publication Data
A CIP record is available from the British Library.

Printed in the United States of America
First Edition

To our families, Bill, Caleb, Gabriel, and Susannah (Lisa's)
and Michael, Adam, and Rachel (Deborah's), with all our love.

Contents

Series Foreword

Contemporary society is marked by a great number of critical challenges: The number of children and families living in poverty is rising. High school dropouts from our nation's schools are increasing, and high-stakes testing is changing the way our students are being educated. We are living with the effects of welfare reform and need to look critically at how these reforms have affected children, youth, and families. Head Start programs, long celebrated for being scientifically based educational interventions, are at risk for losing funding.

Since September 11, 2001, we have lived with new restrictions on our freedoms, new costs for wars launched in the Middle East, and constant fear. How is this new anxiety affecting women who have long been the transmitters of culture and community? Mental health problems in this age of anxiety are enormous even as managed care and federal policies reduce support for mental health services. How can prevention programs be developed in an age of drastic budget cuts and removal of basic social and health services? New neurological research and the genome project are revealing individual differences that require careful thought regarding the implications for education, socialization, and remediation. While our country is becoming more diverse, tolerance and celebration of diversity are decreasing and reproductive choices are becoming more restricted. How are individual rights preserved while we balance human rights and the welfare of others?

Feminist psychologists have claimed they have a moral imperative to improve society. This book and others to follow in the Society for the Psychology of Women Series (Division 35) of the American Psychological Association draw on the expertise of psychologists who have been working on social issues using the lens of feminist consciousness. Forthcoming books in the series will present invited monographs that address critical issues facing our society. These volumes will be based on current scholarship but will be written in a way that is accessible to laypersons who are not knowledgeable in a given field. Longer than a journal article but shorter than a full text, these invited monographs in the series will not just tell the readers *what we know* on a topic, but also what we as a society (as professionals, parents, researchers, policymakers, and citizens) *need to do* regarding the issue.

Mary M. Brabeck, PhD
Book Series Editor
Steinhardt School, New York University

Foreword

Judith L. Herman

Some time ago, I attended the 25th anniversary celebration for a local battered women's shelter. Several of the founders were there to be honored. These were grassroots activists who, back in the 1970s, had opened their homes to shelter women in crisis. Through informal neighborhood networks they had put out the word that their doors would be open when a porch light was on. Eventually this pioneering group succeeded in raising the money for a building to be used as a safe house and organizing volunteers to serve as the shelter staff. The shelter had grown and developed many innovative services. Over time the founding group had been replaced by a more professional staff. Most recently, the shelter had hired a director whose background was in the corporate world as a professional fundraiser. The new staff members brought a wealth of knowledge and skill in their areas of expertise, but they came from a very different class background from that of the founders, and they lacked the founders' intimate knowledge of the community. The 25th anniversary celebration paid tribute to the founders with nostalgia for an era that had passed.

Since its origins more than 30 years ago, the battered women's movement has been remarkably successful. Paradoxically, this means that it has lost some of the qualities of a social change movement. Services for battered women have become institutionalized. This book attempts to com-

Judith L. Herman is training director for the Victims of Violence Program in the Department of Psychiatry of the Cambridge Health Alliance in Cambridge, Massachusetts, and clinical professor of psychiatry at Harvard Medical School, Cambridge, Massachusetts.

bine professional expertise with the passion and spirit of the movement in its early days. The authors are particularly well situated to realize this ambition. Both are distinguished academic scholars, Lisa Goodman as a researcher in clinical and community psychology and Deborah Epstein as a law professor. Both are also devoted activists in the battered women's movement, and both have been part of the movement for more than 20 years, long enough to have known the time when an egalitarian vision of sisterhood was the movement's inspiration and a social analysis of oppression under patriarchy was its common intellectual source.

In the early days of feminist consciousness raising, it was generally understood, as the slogan went, that there were "no individual solutions" to the problem of women's condition. This meant an attitude of tolerance and respect for individual women's choices and compromises, because all choices were seen as compromised. Take, for example, the fact that a majority of women leaving domestic violence shelters return to their partners, either immediately or within a month or two (see pp. 97–98, this volume). This might be understood as a general reflection of women's subordinate economic and social status or as a reflection of the high value women generally place on intimate partner relationships. It never would have been considered a sign of an individual woman's psychopathology. Goodman and Epstein invite their readers to return to a time when women fleeing violence at home were seen as "sisters" rather than "clients" or "cases" and when the success of crisis intervention was judged according to "woman-centered" criteria defined by each individual, not according to any single standard.

Along with feminist insight, Goodman and Epstein bring practical experience based on their long immersion in the day-to-day work of the movement. Out of this experience comes an abundance of concrete and specific policy recommendations for the advocacy, mental health, and justice systems.

Some of these suggestions represent a significant departure from current practices. For example, at present, the great majority of battered women's shelters are at hidden locations. Women seeking shelter are routinely referred to locations far from their familiar neighborhoods, and once they enter a shelter they may be required to cut off contact with the people closest to them for security reasons. Though it may seem counterintuitive, Goodman and Epstein suggest that community-based shelters whose addresses are known to the public may actually be as safe (or as unsafe) as hidden shelters, and they argue that shelters operating in the open might be preferable because they would allow residents to maintain their community ties during their stay.

Turning to the justice system, the authors again draw on their long experience for their policy recommendations. Deborah Epstein was an organizer of one of the first specialized domestic violence courts, in Washington, DC. This has become a model that is now widely imitated, and as these courts are studied carefully, the advantages they offer become apparent. A recent article in the journal *Violence Against Women* reported in depth on one such court in South Carolina.[1] Ninety percent of the victims interviewed reported feeling that the court gave them adequate time to explain their side of the story, and 88% felt they were treated with respect and dignity by the court (and so, it is interesting to note, did a majority of the defendants). The court staff members were described as dedicated and highly engaged. One court investigator explained the satisfaction she felt with her job: "The thing I like about it when I deal with the victims, they tell me 'No one has ever listened to me before. No one has ever believed me.'. . . Those are the things that make it worth it to me" (p. 616). This is a good example of an institutional reform that offers more victims a voice.

When battered women are empowered, all those who participate in the process are enlivened and inspired. This is as true today as it was in the early days of the movement. Women's liberation has been called the "longest revolution."[2] The words "no one has ever listened to me before" have a timeless quality. Those who work with battered women in the advocacy, mental health, and justice systems know that ending violence against women is a long struggle. This book, with its many strategies for empowering battered women, is a source of inspiration for carrying the movement forward.

---

[1] Gover, A. R., Brank, E. M., & MacDonald, J. M. (2007). A specialized domestic violence court in South Carolina: An example of procedural justice for victims and defendants. *Violence Against Women, 13,* 603–626.

[2] Mitchell, J. (1984). *Women, the longest revolution: Essays on feminism, literature, and psychoanalysis.* New York: Pantheon.

Preface

Through the efforts of advocates and activists, the field of domestic violence has witnessed substantial reform, at an almost unprecedentedly rapid pace. But, put simply, existing responses to intimate partner violence are not working well enough. We are increasingly concerned about the ways in which public and private systems are still failing to meet the needs of domestic violence victims. Twenty years ago, we hoped to see wholesale change in existing programs and social institutions, yet this has not come to pass. Even where dramatic positive change has occurred, unintended negative consequences have often followed. Particularly for battered women who are poor, immigrants, members of minority cultures or racial groups, in same-sex relationships, or who choose to remain in abusive relationships, current mainstream interventions actually may do more harm than good by failing to respond sufficiently to a woman's individual needs. As one example, the prosecution of a batterer may disrupt a survivor's family and community ties, place her at risk of retaliatory violence, and deprive her of crucial sources of income.

It is far from clear that there has been any major reduction in the incidence or prevalence of intimate partner violence in this country over the past few decades, despite substantial efforts to improve systemic responses to the problem. Little evidence exists to support the effectiveness of many mainstream and widespread interventions in systems that range from criminal justice to mental health to temporary shelter, and many domestic violence victims have little access to, or use for, existing services. It is now time for the field as a whole to take stock. We need to critically examine where we have been and begin a discussion about how future responses to partner violence can both be more effective and embrace a broader range of survivors. That is what we have set out to do in this book.

We have tried to structure this book to facilitate discussion among a wide range of audiences. We apply our essential critique—that it is time to move beyond the one-size-fits-all rigid responses that marginalize women's particular situations and perspectives—across disciplines (psychology and law) and across systems (advocacy, mental health, and justice). This integrated perspective allows us to paint a more comprehensive and richer picture of societal responses to battered women and future opportunities for reform. We also attempt to address the interests of a variety of potential readers. We hope that this book is a useful text in a wide range of university courses that reflect on women's lives; that it also may serve as a thought-provoking guide for those interested in becoming advocates, counselors, therapists, or lawyers for survivors of intimate partner violence; and finally, that it offers experienced practitioners a framework for debate and activism promoting new approaches for ensuring battered women's physical and psychological safety.

Consistent with our theme—the need for increased responsiveness to the particular concerns of individual women—we have made our best efforts to listen to and build on the stories and experiences of battered women and those who work closely with them. We analyze these stories, as well as the responses of the advocacy, mental health, and justice systems, from the perspectives of feminist theory and feminist psychology.

Given the broad scope and depth of domestic violence research and scholarship, it is important to state explicitly what we, as coauthors, have to contribute to the discussion. Each of us has worked with and for survivors of partner abuse for more than 20 years. In collaboration with many others, we have written articles, developed programs, designed new public–private systems, and spent time with women who have experienced violence in their most intimate relationships.

Lisa is a clinical and community psychologist who has conducted research on the psychological impact of intimate partner violence on marginalized women, including those who are poor, severely mentally ill, or homeless. She has explored how such violence shapes women's mental health over time; how women strategize to keep themselves safe; and how their social networks, communities, and local institutions respond to these efforts. Over the past few years, she has collaborated on the development of new community-based and court-based programs that respond to battered women in individualized, empowering, and context-sensitive ways.

Deborah is an attorney and law professor who helped lead an effort to design and implement one of the nation's first specialized domestic violence courts in Washington, DC. The court integrates civil and criminal justice system responses to domestic violence victims, perpetrators, and their children. Her scholarship analyzes contemporary efforts to reform systemic responses to those in abusive relationships and suggests new ways to improve the legal system. She has put many of her ideas into practice through the work of the Domestic Violence Clinic at Georgetown University Law Center, which she directs.

We found each other 10 years ago when we both joined a domestic violence fatality review committee in Washington, DC, designed to conduct detailed investigations of local domestic violence-related murders. Since then, we have collaborated on numerous programmatic and research projects.

Over the years, we both have had the privilege of working with advocates, mental health professionals, and justice system participants who, despite system-based restrictions and limited resources, transform battered women's lives through constant heroic acts. There are also many people, too numerous to mention individually, whose ideas we have become familiar with through our scholarship and by listening to and learning from others at conferences and on LISTSERV discussions. We are indebted to so many of these thoughtful individuals for their tireless work to keep women safe from abuse at the hands of their intimate partners.

As we wrote this book, we asked several people for brutally honest readings (and sometimes rereadings) of the manuscript, and all of them came through. For helping us avoid our worst impulses and fuzziest thinking, our enormous thanks go to Victoria Banyard, Margret Bell, Lauren Bennett Cattaneo, Carrie Epstein, Juley Fulcher, Frank and Joan Goodman, Margaret Johnson, Catherine Klein, Laurie Kohn, Leslie Lebowitz, Elizabeth Liu, Susan Marine, Joan Meier, Danielle Pelfrey Duryea, Michael Shuman, Katya Fels Smyth, Bill Weinreb, Janet Yassen, and Robin Zachary.

We were fortunate to have many research assistants over the course of this project, whose substantive ideas and research, as well as help with fact and citation checking, were invaluable. We thank Angela Borges, Catherine Glenn, Rachel Latta, Lori Mihalich, Danielle Pelfrey Duryea, Jennifer Toussant, and Sarah Weintraub.

For both of us, the ideas that we explore here have been influenced, directly and indirectly, by a large group of colleagues and mentors (some of whom may not be aware of it). We thank Laura Brown, Jacquelyn Campbell, Jill Davies, Mary Ann Dutton, Edward Gondolf, Barbara Hart, Mary Koss, Eleanor Lyon, Diane Monti-Catania, Jody Raphael, Beth Richie, Susan Schechter, Evan Stark, Cris Sullivan, Lenore Walker, Laurie Woods, and Joan Zorza. We are especially grateful to Judy Herman, whose ideas have inspired us both throughout our careers, and we are honored that she has written the foreword for this book.

From Lisa, special thanks go to Deborah Belle, Sarah Cook, David Ford, Mary Harvey, Angela Littwin, Belle Liang, Nancy Ryan, and the women of Reach Out About Depression (ROAD).

From Deborah, special thanks go to Jane Aiken, Claudia Angelos, Margaret Martin Barry, Joanna Bond, Sue Bryant, Donna Coker, Sharon Denaro, Norman Dorsen, Bea Epstein, Stephen Epstein, Daniel Filler, Juley Fulcher, Suzanne Jackson, Vicki Jackson, Westley Jackson (who inspired me to rethink everything), Margaret Johnson, Ayesha Khan, Catherine Klein, Tammy Kuennen, Sylvia Law, Ann Shalleck, Anne Schroth, Joan Meier, Nancy Meyer, Leslye Orloff, Jon Rapping, Elizabeth Schneider, Robert Spagnoletti, Nadine Strossen, Harry Subin, Robin West, Wendy Williams, and all of the clients of the Georgetown University Law Center's Domestic Violence Clinic.

Finally, we deeply appreciate the support of our partners. They suffered endless hours discussing minutiae, repeatedly screwed up the courage to tell us to go back to the drawing board, and were enormously patient in rereading chapter after chapter.

Bill, your intellectual clarity and impatience with obscuring jargon have kept me honest while your irreverence and good humor have kept me sane. In this as in all things, your companionship has sustained me. Thank you.

—Lisa

Michael, your intellectual honesty, integrity, passion, and boundless curiosity inspire everyone around you to greater depth and clarity of thought. I owe so many of my accomplishments to your inspiration, challenge, and support; I am truly grateful.

—Deborah

Introduction

Nearly one quarter of the women in this country are physically or sexually assaulted by an intimate partner (Tjaden & Thoennes, 2000). They are slapped, shoved, kicked, punched, beaten, and choked. They are stalked, threatened, and humiliated. They are isolated from friends and family, constantly monitored, thwarted in their efforts to work, and told that they are worthless.

This is as true now as it was in the early 1970s, when feminist activists in the United States successfully brought the issue of intimate partner violence to public notice. Since then, domestic violence has seized the attention of advocates, researchers, and policymakers. Legal and legislative reforms have substantially expanded the options available to battered women; researchers have shed light on the prevalence, causes, and consequences of domestic violence; and front-line service providers have worked to ensure victim safety, offender accountability, and community awareness. This book explores these reforms through an in-depth examination of three different areas: the domestic violence advocacy community, the mental health profession, and the justice system. Other institutional and systemic responses to intimate partner violence exist, including those emerging from religious institutions, the health care professions, and employment settings. However, because the three areas identified are the most extensive and furthest developed at this point in time, we center our analysis on them and explore why they have not had a greater impact.

WHY EMPHASIZE SOCIETAL RESPONSES?

We have chosen to focus this book specifically on our society's responses to domestic violence because we understand the problem as a social one rather than as a problem of aberrant or pathological individuals. Despite early attempts by feminist advocates to highlight the fundamental political and social determinants of partner violence, much research has focused on the personal characteristics of victims and perpetrators. Although such research has yielded important information, it also has contributed to the widespread belief that intimate partner violence is rooted in individual pathology rather than in gender-based power hierarchies and the societal norms and institutions that support and reinforce women's subordination. Although a wide range of personal and familial factors affect the odds that a particular man will commit an act of domestic violence, the dominance of male power in our culture facilitates and legitimizes such violence. Our analysis leads us to advocate solutions that entail fundamental change in both our public agencies and in civil society.

A FEMINIST PERSPECTIVE

We approach this book from a feminist perspective. As we analyze historic and contemporary responses to intimate partner violence—topics we consider essential for those unfamiliar with the field—we emphasize the insights and critiques that feminist theory and feminist psychology have to offer.

Feminist theory encompasses a wide variety of perspectives, all of which stem from the fundamental insight that gender is an essential component of every individual's lived experiences. Feminist theories attempt to describe women's varied experiences of subordination, analyze the causes and consequences, and prescribe strategies for future change. Our thinking about domestic violence has relied in large part on four essential principles that are common to a wide range of feminist philosophical perspectives (for a more in-depth discussion of these, see Ballou, 2005; M. Brabeck & Brown, 1997; Hill & Ballou, 2005).

First, feminist theorizing is by nature a political enterprise, with the goal of social transformation (Chamallas, 1999; hooks, 1984). This book aims not only to describe our society's response to domestic violence but also to help readers critically evaluate recent reform efforts. As feminist scholar Chamallas (1999) put it, "Change does not always mean progress . . . basic gender hierarchies can survive attempts at reform and . . . patterns of inequality [can be] reproduced in different and updated forms" (pp. 2–3). We set out our ideas for change in the hope that this book will serve as a catalyst for progress on behalf of survivors.

Second, feminist theory tends to flow from women's experiences. Feminist responses to social problems often are based on careful nonjudgmental listening to and valuing of individual women's voices, especially those of women most likely to be silenced by existing social forces. As we analyze the domestic violence literature, we attempt to give voice to the hundreds of individual survivors who have spoken to us over the years. We do so in part through explicit storytelling. Many of the stories told here are based on our personal experiences working with many clients in the justice and mental health systems. Others are drawn from vignettes published by other researchers and scholars. The names of all participants have been changed to protect their privacy and, in some instances, attorney–client or client–therapist privilege. Occasionally, minor identifying details have been altered to further protect survivor privacy.

Finally, feminist theory relies heavily on the insight that a woman's individual personal experience tends to be rooted in complex social realities. Our discussion emphasizes the ways in which societal transformation can be a prerequisite or at least a corequisite to a survivor's ability to accomplish individual change.

Although gender is a critical force shaping women's opportunities and experiences, its impact is modulated by its intersection with other self- and socially defining characteristics, such as ethnicity, culture, class, age, sexual orientation, ability, immigration status, and personal history. A focus on gender alone fails to illuminate the crucial impact of these other defining aspects of women's lives. Although we limit our discussion to battered women (as opposed to male victims) we understand that survivors of partner violence are not a monolithic group but a diverse collection of individuals from a variety of ethnic, racial, and socioeconomic backgrounds.

Recent reforms have dramatically expanded the practical options available to many battered women, but they have simultaneously sacrificed much of the contextualized, woman-centered focus that existed in the early years of the anti–domestic violence movement. To capitalize on the substantial gains achieved over the past 30 years and to move beyond the losses that have accompanied them, those of us who work with and for battered women must return three major feminist themes to the movement's central focus.

First, battered women's individual voices need to be brought back to the forefront of reform efforts. Those who are attempting to help battered women must honor the differences in their individual needs by creating opportunities for their voices to be heard and for them to play an active role in shaping the assistance they receive. In the early years of the battered women's movement, feminist activists encouraged women to find their individual voices and tell their personal stories. Early domestic violence advocates focused on creating collaborative relationships with survivors in which a woman defined and controlled her own path to safety. However, recent reform efforts have shifted substantially away from this focus on battered women's individual voices. Today, services tend to require survivors to fit their situations into predefined categories, even when their circumstances are quite complex, with the abuse representing just one problem among many. Battered women whose needs do not mesh neatly with available services may receive no assistance or may feel pressure to accept help that only poorly suits their needs or is even contrary to their interests (Davies, Lyon, & Monti-Catania, 1998). This separation of the battered women's movement from core feminist tradition has substantially limited possibilities for victim empowerment.

Second, we need to recognize the critical importance of women's community ties and individual relationships. Although connection to others is essential to the physical safety and psychological recovery of most battered women, existing services frequently fail to promote connection and often actively undermine it. As one example, for a variety of reasons shelters typically are located at confidential addresses, distant from their clients' families, friends, and communities. A battered woman resident may be barred from divulging her temporary address or phone number, and she may be cut off from potential sources of support during a time of crisis. We should consider alternative models that provide shelter to battered women within their geographic, cultural, and other communities. Further, service providers need to find ways to help isolated battered women reconnect with, expand, and strengthen supportive social networks or create new ones.

In addition to promoting community, we must recognize the importance of individual relationships to many battered women. Therapists, police, prosecutors, and judges typically assume that the only acceptable choice for a survivor is to separate from her partner. However, recent data demonstrate that staying may be the safer option for some victims. Still, when a woman expresses a desire to be safe but also to remain in her relationship, system actors are increasingly likely to substitute their own judgment for hers, encouraging or even coercing her to leave. The result is that many women avoid shelters and the criminal justice system altogether, and the potential benefits of these resources are seriously undermined. We need to develop the flexibility to accept a woman's decision to continue her connection with an abusive partner while always ensuring she has the opportunity to exit if she chooses to do so.

Third, as we expand the options available to battered women, we should focus particularly on those whose socioeconomic status limits their opportunities to achieve safety. The anti–domestic violence movement as a whole has been relatively slow to recognize the crucial role played by poverty in battered women's lives. Current responses to domestic violence pay far too little attention to the importance of providing impoverished victims with financial assistance and helping them to achieve economic autonomy. The political commitment to the slogan "domestic violence crosses all socioeconomic lines" has interfered with efforts to work toward the economic empowerment of those victims with fewest alternatives. Research now shows that poverty is a crucial facilitating factor in the occurrence of domestic violence and that it severely limits a woman's chances to be safe. Without a strong focus on economic empowerment, reform efforts for victims of partner violence cannot be fully successful.

CHAPTER OVERVIEW

Chapter 1 discusses the reasons to prioritize domestic violence as a social issue. We describe the enormity of the problem in terms of its prevalence and impact, not only on victims themselves but also on their families, communities, and society. In chapters 2 through 4, we review the evolution of our society's treatment of domestic violence over time, describing reform efforts in the fields of advocacy, mental health, and civil and criminal justice. In chapter 5, we articulate a critique that applies across all of these systems: It is time to move beyond the one-size-fits-all responses that fail to account for a battered woman's individual situation. The rigid policies that dominate the field reveal how individuals and institutions that respond to intimate partner violence have abandoned or ignored the three basic principles of listening to individual women's voices, promoting supportive communities, and facilitating economic empowerment. We discuss how a renewed focus on these principles could result in substantial future progress. Finally, in chapter 6, we make a series of concrete recommendations for improvements in the advocacy, mental health, and justice systems.

The Need for Continued Reform: The Broad Scope and Deep Impact of Intimate Partner Violence

At a recent police academy training on domestic violence issues, an officer spoke up:

> You're telling us about all of these new laws and changes in the system that are supposed to help victims of domestic violence. But I've been around, and even though I know there are some really bad situations out there, lots of the domestic violence calls I respond to end up being a situation where the husband slapped his wife a couple of times, or maybe punched her. I'm not saying I have no sympathy for her, but lots of times they've got kids together and they really need to just work things out. There's a lot of serious crime out there; do we really need to keep coming up with more special policies for domestic violence? Haven't we done enough?[1]

This comment is not atypical. It illustrates contemporary attitudes held by many judges, prosecutors, police officers, and even some mental health professionals and private service providers. After all, some incidents of intimate partner abuse do involve relatively low-level violence, particularly when compared with the kind of violence common on inner-city streets. And those working to end domestic violence already have received

---

[1] This comment was made to one of the authors by an anonymous Washington, DC, police officer during a presentation at a DC Metropolitan Police Department Training Academy session on domestic violence in October 2001.

extensive legislative attention, federal funding, and judicial focus. As described in chapters 2 through 4, the battered women's movement has made substantial progress in raising awareness of the problem and developing an array of responses in the advocacy, mental health, and civil and criminal justice systems.

So why prioritize partner violence as a focus for further reform? This chapter begins to answer that question by examining the extent and impact of domestic violence at this moment in history. Domestic abuse continues to be an enormous social problem, with devastating consequences for women, their families, and their communities. Despite all of the progress that has been made, responses to partner violence remain inadequate. In addition, many recent reform efforts have created new, unintended challenges of their own. The continuing pervasiveness of and damage caused by intimate partner violence make clear that creative new approaches still are desperately needed.

WOMEN AS VICTIMS

This book focuses on women victimized by male partners. This was neither an easy nor an obvious decision. The debate on "gender symmetry"— whether women use violence in their intimate relationships as frequently as do men—has continued full tilt since 1980, when the highly publicized and controversial first National Family Violence Survey was published (Straus, Gelles, & Steinmetz, 1980). The survey, based on a national probability sample, demonstrated that rates of wife-to-husband assault were slightly higher than rates of husband-to-wife assault. These findings, which were largely confirmed by a second national survey (the National Family Violence Resurvey; Straus & Gelles, 1990), triggered 20 years of divisive debate over the role of gender in domestic violence (Frieze, 2005). In subsequent years, several prevalence studies confirmed these results, whereas others showed men as disproportionately likely to be perpetrators and women to be victims (e.g., Tjaden & Thoennes, 2000). The debate was further fueled by research that demonstrated that lesbian couples also experience partner violence, giving additional support to the role of women as perpetrators as well as victims (Merrill & Wolfe, 2000; Renzetti, 1992).

This controversy extended beyond the research community to popular culture. In 1999, Oprah Winfrey produced a show on "Wives Who Abuse Their Husbands"; in 1997, *20/20* ran a segment entitled "Battered by Their Wives"; and in 2003, the Boston Globe ran the headline, "In Abuse, Men Are Victims Too" (Young, 2003). Public officials have devoted resources to dealing with women's violence, with women now comprising a significant proportion (between 12% and 31%, depending on the state) of those arrested for domestic offenses (DeLeon-Granados, Wells, & Binsbacher, 2006; Hirschel & Buzawa, 2002). Emerging gender symmetry findings have led some scholars and activists to argue that the "old" feminist view of domestic violence as a consequence of socially constructed and culturally approved gender inequality, with men as the perpetrators and women as the victims, is outdated and incorrect (Hamel, 2005; Straus, 2006).

Recent research has put some of this controversy to rest. Much of the gender symmetry debate can be resolved by distinguishing between "intimate terrorism" and "situational couple violence" (M. P. Johnson, 1995, 2006; M. P. Johnson & Ferraro, 2000). In *intimate terrorism* relationships, the perpetrator engages in a general pattern of coercion and control over his partner—over her finances, social contacts, everyday activities, employment, parenting practices, even the clothes she wears—and uses violence as one means to that end. Even nonviolent control tactics take on a violent meaning through their implicit connection with potential physical harm. This pattern creates a climate of fear that is common to other forms of terrorism as well. The term *situational couple violence*, in contrast, applies to relationships where specific conflicts occasionally escalate into relatively low-level violence, such as slapping or throwing an object at a partner. Although both forms of abuse fall squarely within the category of domestic violence, the former typically results in far more serious physical and emotional harm.

When researchers ask about situational couple violence—that is, violence in the context of partner conflict—results suggest gender symmetry. In contrast, when they ask about intimate terrorism—violence in the context of coercive control—they reveal far higher rates of male-perpetrated violence (Kimmel, 2002; Stark, 2006). One study in Britain, for example, found that 87% of violence that occurs in intimate terrorism relationships was perpetrated by men, compared with 45% of situational couple violence (Graham-Kevan & Archer, 2003). Another large survey in the United States showed that women were over 8 times more likely to be stalked than were men. The study also found that violence perpetrated against women was more likely to be accompanied by signs of intimate terrorism, such as emotionally abusive and controlling behavior, than was violence against men (Tjaden & Thoennes, 2000).

Victims of intimate terrorism, in contrast to less severe forms of abuse, are more likely to be injured, to exhibit more symptoms of post-traumatic stress, and to leave their partners (Johnson & Leone, 2005). Male perpetrators of intimate terrorism appear to have far more misogynistic attitudes than do nonviolent men or perpetrators of situational couple violence (Holzworth-Munroe, Meehan, Herron, Rehman, & Stuart, 2000). The following example illustrates some of the central patterns in such relationships.

> When Judy met Tom, she was enrolled in college part time and worked as a server at a local restaurant. She was close to her family and had strong friendships. Tom was a successful local business owner and a respected community member. He was romantic; he took her on extravagant vacations and surprised her with gifts. A year after they met, they married. One month into the marriage, Tom suggested that Judy quit her job at the restaurant so that she could focus on her school work. He insisted that he could pay their bills and that her job was unnecessary. She told him she enjoyed earning money for herself and liked working with her friends at the restaurant. Tom accepted this response at first but soon started questioning her about the clothes she wore to work, telling her it looked like she was trying to get attention from other men. She assured him she was not. He insisted that if she really loved him, she would change her clothing style. Tom also forbade her to talk about this discussion with her friends, because this was a private matter.

She wondered if this was what marriage was supposed to be like and wished she could talk about it, but she loved him and decided to try to do as he asked.

A month later, Judy found Tom in a rage about the speedometer on her car. He had calculated the number of miles she should have driven to commute to and from work and concluded that she had been surreptitiously seeing another man. Tom threatened that if she did not quit her job, he would stop paying their bills. When she protested and assured him that she would never be unfaithful, he cornered her in their bedroom and locked the door. He said that he would not let her out until she called and quit her job. After she made the call, Tom apologized, saying he only wanted what was best for her and he would not act that way again. The next day, he bought her flowers. She felt a little better, but things only got worse. Tom began interrupting her while she was studying, insisting that she have sex with him. Once, when she refused, he locked her in the bedroom and raped her. When she tried to escape by jumping out the window, he wrestled her to the ground and tied her hands together. He held a kitchen knife in his hand and told Judy that if she tried to escape again, he would stab her. Judy began failing her courses. She was terrified and felt ashamed about what was happening in her marriage. Tom kept insisting that if she would be a good wife, she would be happy.

Soon Tom was limiting Judy to a small "allowance" for her expenses and monitoring her financial transactions. When she tried to get support from her friends and family, he said they would not believe her because he was so well-respected in the community. He threatened that if she spoke to them about anything he would tie her up, stab her, and go after them. Judy stayed away from her friends and family because she feared for their safety—and for her own. On the few occasions when she argued or attempted to defy Tom, he punched her but always in a place where she could cover it up. Although these incidents of violence were rare, the threat was always in the air. After being married to Tom for 2 years, Judy had essentially become a prisoner in her own home. She was disconnected from her friends and family. She had lost her job and dropped out of college.

She had no money and, seemingly, no options (A. Borges, personal communication, October 10, 2006).[2]

Although this book attempts to address the broad sweep of intimate partner violence, victims of intimate terrorism are those most likely to be seen in our health, mental health, and justice systems (Lloyd & Taluc, 1999; Zweig, Burt, & Van Ness, 2003), and on whom, therefore, most research has focused. Far less is known about patterns of situational couple violence.

Despite our focus on violence committed by men against women, we do not wish to minimize the significance of violence in same-sex relationships. Research over the past decade indicates that such violence is as prevalent and harmful as violence in heterosexual relationships (Gunther & Jennings, 1999; McClennen, 2005; Merrill & Wolfe, 2000). At the same time, same-sex violence—where women are perpetrators (as well as victims) and men are victims (as well as perpetrators)—may not fit into typical patterns of abuse in heterosexual relationships and raises additional complex issues. Although we decided that we would not be able to do justice, in the context of this book, to issues of domestic violence in the gay and lesbian community, where possible, we have highlighted how system actors can be more responsive to the critical needs of this neglected population.

TERMS AND DEFINITIONS

Any discussion of domestic violence must begin by clarifying the terms used to describe the problem of one partner hurting another in the context of an intimate relationship. Terms like *family violence, courtship violence, domestic violence, spousal abuse, marital violence,* and *intimate partner violence* have been used interchangeably but often mean different things in different contexts. The plethora of terms and meanings frequently causes researchers and policymakers to talk past, rather than to, each other and has deeply undermined opportunities to learn from past work. In the late 1990s, the Centers for Disease Control and Prevention

---

[2] This is the story of a resident at a New Hampshire shelter, as told to an advocate who worked there.

(CDC) attempted to remedy this problem by creating a panel of experts to develop recommendations for consistency in research terminology. In 1999, the agency published a set of guidelines that defined intimate partner violence to encompass physical and sexual violence, threats of physical and sexual violence, and psychological and emotional abuse that occur in the context of prior physical or sexual violence (Saltzman, Fanslow, McMahon, & Shelley, 1999). The CDC adopted the term *intimate partner violence* to describe this type of abuse because it was narrow enough to differentiate between partners and other family relationships yet expansive enough to include all partnerships, regardless of marital status or sexual orientation (McClennen, 2005). The definition does, however, leave out certain culture-specific types of abuse—acts that can be as traumatizing as actual violence, depending on their cultural meanings. By Japanese standards, for example, shaming a woman by dousing her with liquid to connote that she is impure or contaminated can be experienced as more abusive than acts of violence such as pushing, grabbing, or slapping (Sokoloff & Dupont, 2005b).

In this book, we adopt the CDC's definition of intimate partner violence, which is slowly becoming the standard in the field, but we also use several other terms for such violence interchangeably (including *partner violence* and *domestic violence*). We also use the terms *physical abuse, sexual abuse,* and *psychological abuse* to denote specific types of violence where relevant.

Controversy also surrounds the terms used to describe someone who experiences intimate partner violence. Some have used terms such as *victim, survivor,* and *battered woman* interchangeably. However, others argue that these terms mean distinctly different things, with the word *victim* implying that a person is still enduring abuse or its consequences, *survivor* implying that she has moved past the damaging effects of abuse, and *battered woman* indicating the severity of domestic violence and its gendered nature. In this book, we have chosen to use these terms interchangeably, consistent with our observation from experience that a woman can move fluidly between an identity as victim and an identity as survivor—between seeing herself as someone who has endured a horrific experience and someone who has survived with strength. To choose one term over the others prioritizes one of these identities when, in fact, all reflect important aspects of the intimate partner violence experience.

EXTENT OF INTIMATE PARTNER VIOLENCE IN THE UNITED STATES

In 1980, Murray Straus and his colleagues (Straus, Gelles, & Steinmetz, 1980) published their landmark national survey, which showed that one out of eight husbands had committed at least one violent act against his wife during the year of the study. "With the exception of the police and the military," the authors concluded, "the family is perhaps the most violent social group, and the home is the most violent social setting in our society" (p. 15). Shocking as it was, the one-in-eight figure failed to capture the risk of partner violence over a woman's lifetime.

Numerous other studies have confirmed the extraordinarily high rates of domestic violence in this country, not only among married couples, but also among those who are cohabitating, dating, in a same-sex relationship, or whose relationships have ended. The largest and most recent of these studies was the 1995–1996 National Violence Against Women Survey (NVAWS), sponsored jointly by the National Institute of Justice and the Centers for Disease Control and Prevention, in which 16,000 men and women were asked about their exposure to a wide range of partner violence–related behaviors, including sexual violence, emotional and psychological abuse, stalking, and physical violence (Tjaden & Thoennes, 2000). Using a definition of *physical assault* that included a range of behaviors from slapping to hitting to using a gun and a definition of *rape* that included forced vaginal, oral, and anal intercourse, the survey found that nearly 25% of women, compared with 8% of men, had been raped or physically assaulted by a current or former spouse, cohabitating partner, or date at some point in their lives. Eleven percent of women cohabitating with women had experienced partner violence, compared with 30% of women cohabitating with men.

The true prevalence of partner violence is undoubtedly higher than even these numbers suggest. Because the NVAWS was conducted through telephone interviews, it excluded low-income women without phones, women living on the streets or with friends, and women in hospitals or other institutions, all of whom typically report higher rates of violence than those who are more economically stable (Browne & Bassuk, 1997; Goodman, Fels, & Glenn, 2006). Women living in households with annual incomes below $10,000 are 4 times more likely to be violently attacked, most often by intimates, than women with higher income levels (Kaplan, 1997). A 1995 national study found that household income level was the single most important predictor of partner violence (Cunradi, Caetano, & Schafer, 2002; for an in-depth discussion of the complex relationship between poverty and domestic violence, see chap. 5, this volume).

The NVAWS also found differences in prevalence across ethnic groups, with White women reporting significantly less partner violence than African American and Native American women but more than Asian American and Pacific Islander women and approximately the same partner violence as Latinas. These differences disappear, however, after controlling for socioeconomic factors (A. L. Coker et al., 2002; Rennison & Planty, 2003). Similarly, studies have shown that male unemployment explains differences in domestic homicide rates that initially seemed to be related to race (Campbell et al., 2003). It thus appears that poverty, unemployment, and other social and structural disadvantages are at the root of apparent ethnic differences in prevalence of partner violence, probably because low-income women lack many crucial resources necessary to protect themselves or to escape from abusive situations (see chap. 5, this volume).

As sobering as these statistics are, they cannot convey the trauma of being physically hurt, humiliated, intimidated, and controlled by someone with whom one has an intimate relationship, and the statistics mean little to a woman living with the aftermath of domestic violence. "Clara's" story offers a concrete illustration of the reality of a survivor's life. (This and many other real-life survivor stories were compiled in an amicus brief submitted to the U.S. Supreme Court, in the case of *Davis v. Washington* [2006]; see Brief for the National Network to End Domestic Violence, 2006.)

> My story covers . . . a span of almost 20 years. . . . My abuse began in
> 1988. While some incidents may have been seen as borderline, sev-

eral were obvious abuse—a broken nose, cracked jaw, numerous bruises—usually around the neck. Before the births of the children that we share, born in 1991 and 1992, I [did not testify against my abusive partner in court] because of his threats to me—afterward this included threats regarding the children. I was not stupid or uneducated. . . . [I]t all started so gradually that I did not see the cocoon of helplessness and no-contact that he had enveloped me in.

I had gradually been cut off from friends and family so that I truly believed I had no one to help, and as in the case of some abusers, mine had friendships with some of the police. He left me with three young children . . . but insisted that I remain faithful to him as he lived with and dated several other women. As I could not afford to work and pay daycare, I was reduced to living on welfare—and he used this against me also. He stole what little money I had on many occasions, raped me and beat me on several occasions.

When the police would come, he would laugh and state, "you know these welfare women," and they would laugh along with him. Even with prodding from medical staff, I almost always refused to testify—if the police wouldn't believe me who would?

Things began to change when I found an at-home study program to finish my degree. I talked with professors at the university. . . . I made new friends, and old friends and family began to renew their faith in me. My parents helped me locate to a new town, almost 200 miles away. . . . [I]t only helped somewhat—he continued to try to pursue me with threats about the children.

The last time he beat me was in November of 1994—and I am shaking even now as I recall it. I told him "no," in no uncertain terms, "no." I would not do this anymore. Our children were at daycare, and in my new location, I had found assistance to work part-time and go to school. The "no" was met with quite a beating. He truly tried to kill me. In an instant of the madness, when I could barely walk—(at this time I had broken ribs and severe swelling and bruising around the throat)—I pretended to vomit—my abuser's weakness was a bad stomach—as he turned to face the other direction, I went for the second-story window as quickly as I could. I didn't make it—he caught my arms on the sill—but I screamed and yelled enough to get the attention of neighbors. It still didn't stop completely. He explained to neighbors it was just a spat and pulled me in broken and bruised and bleeding—and pulled all the phones from the plugs and made me sit next to him. He gave me the usual threats and then sat there until he knew that I had to pick up the children from daycare so that I would not go to the police or hospital. He followed me to the daycare after making me clean up as best as possible—and left from the daycare. The old me may have listened in fear, but the new me was determined to pursue my new life without fear. [I spoke to the police and eventually he was prosecuted and convicted]. . . . I can't describe the feeling of how it felt, after so long, that someone believed me. (Brief for the National Network to End Domestic Violence, 2006, Appendix B, pp. 65a–68a)

THE IMPACT OF INTIMATE PARTNER VIOLENCE ON WOMEN

The devastating and varied impact of partner violence has been well documented over the past decade. In this section, we consider these data from multiple perspectives, starting with the damage inflicted on a woman's physical and mental health and then turning to the harm radiating out to her personal relationships, broader communities, and the social institutions with which she interacts (Riger, Raja, & Camacho, 2002).

Impact on Physical Health

Domestic abuse is rarely a one-time event and often escalates in severity and frequency, particularly in intimate terrorism relationships (Capaldi, Shortt, & Crosby, 2003; M. P. Johnson & Ferraro, 2000). A woman who seeks help today with a black eye may return a few months later with a permanent bald spot caused by her boyfriend pulling a handful of hair out of her head or with several teeth knocked out by a hammer. A batterer whose actions go unchecked eventually may reach the point where he commits a homicide. For example, in one multicity study that compared abuse cases that ended in homicide with those that did not, a "highly controlling" abuser was one of two risk factors that increased a victim's risk of fatality ninefold (Campbell, Sharps, & Glass, 2000).

Battering by husbands, ex-husbands, or lovers is one of the most common causes of injury to women in the United States (Rand, 1997). These injuries may include sprains, burns, broken teeth and bones, dislocations, damage to internal organs, wounds from knives or guns, and permanent disfigurement or brain damage (Acevedo, 2000; H. Jackson, Philp, Nuttall, & Diller, 2002). Approximately 30% of all murders of women in this country are committed by current or ex-partners (Greenfield et al., 1998; Puzone, 2000; Rennison & Welchans, 2000),[3] and more than 10 murder–suicides occur each week, the vast majority of which are perpetrated by men against women (Violence Policy Center, 2006).

Researchers have found that partner violence has a dose–response effect on health: Increases in the severity of violence produce proportional increases in health problems (Campbell, 2002; Eby, 1996). Injuries caused by partner violence can lead directly to long-term health issues, such as chronic pain, osteoarthritis, and severe headaches (Campbell, 2002; A. L. Coker, Smith, Bethea, King, & McKeown, 2000). Partner violence also can contribute indirectly, through stress, to problems such as sleep difficulties, gastrointestinal problems, and chronic headaches (A. L. Coker et al., 2000; Sutherland, Sullivan, & Bybee, 2001).

The acute and chronic health problems arising from domestic violence can impair a woman's everyday functioning, her interactions with others, and her ability to fulfill critical social roles such as parent, employee, and friend (Browne, Salomon, & Bassuk, 1999).

Impact on Mental Health

In addition to causing physical harm, intimate partner violence also creates serious and long-lasting psychological and emotional injuries, especially when it takes the form of intimate terrorism (Cook & Goodman, 2006; Dutton & Goodman, 2005; Dutton, Goodman, & Bennett, 1999).

---

[3] African American women are murdered by partners at 3 times the rate of White women (Violence Policy Center, 2005).

Most domestic violence victims struggle with low self-esteem; social isolation; and feelings of despair, distrust, hopelessness, and anger (Follingstad, Brennan, Hause, Polek, & Rutledge, 1991; Koss et al., 1994; Riger et al., 2002; Sackett & Saunders, 1999). For many, these feelings become deeply entrenched. Studies show that on average, almost half of partner violence victims suffer from depression (Golding, 1999) compared with 10% to 20% of the general population of women (Kessler et al., 1994; Weissman, Bruce, Leaf, Florio, & Holzer, 1991), and almost 20% struggle with suicidal thoughts and feelings (Golding, 1999). In addition, more than 60% of battered women suffer from posttraumatic stress disorder (PTSD) compared with rates between 1% and 12% in the general population (Breslau, Davis, Andreski, & Peterson, 1991; Davidson, Hughes, Blazer, & George, 1991; Helzer, Robins, & McEvoy, 1987; Kessler, Sonnega, Bromet, Hughes, & Nelson, 1995; Resnick, Kilpatrick, Dansky, Saunders, & Best, 1993). Women experiencing PTSD may have extreme difficulty concentrating, feel constantly on guard and jumpy, and display unpredictable outbursts of rage. When they recall the abuse they have suffered, women with PTSD often have flashbacks that they experience as an actual reliving of the trauma. In the moment, these flashbacks are terrifying and overwhelming. The flashbacks also may be accompanied by night terrors or repeated, intrusive memories, thoughts, or images of traumatic incidents. In reaction, victims typically go to great lengths to avoid situations that remind them of the abuse (American Psychiatric Association, 1994; Dutton et al., 1999). This makes it all but impossible for many domestic violence survivors to obtain assistance from the mental health or criminal justice systems, where they commonly are asked to retell their stories repeatedly and in great detail. For example, as Clara explained,

> Today, even ten years later, after years of counseling to become whole again—I still have a hard time facing [my former partner] in court in matters about the children. Over ten years after my last beating it still makes me throw-up when I have to face him. I break out in a horrible, drenching cold sweat. I shake from the tips of my fingers to toes—which I usually have to consciously place on the ground with force to stop my heels from clacking in the courtroom. Time can heal the wounds from the past, but nothing can stop the fear that I have

of this man. I often have to seek medical attention afterwards for migraines. . . . Fear—not the abuse itself—is the major part of abuse that keeps a victim in their helpless position. . . . That fear has been used as proficiently as any knife or gun might be used by a marksman or hunter. While a true weapon such as a knife or gun may be used as part of the package, the look, the voice, or the words of the abuser serve as just as much a fear stimulator—and those that have been at it for a while are expert fear marksmen. (Brief for the National Network to End Domestic Violence, 2006, Appendix B, pp. 65a–68a)

To avoid the psychological pain of abuse and subsequent PTSD, many battered women attempt to self-medicate through drug and alcohol abuse in an effort to calm themselves, to reduce symptoms of arousal, to block out intrusive thoughts, or to create an overall sense of numbness (Clark & Foy, 2000; Hien & Hien, 1998; S. C. Lemon, Verhoek-Oftedahl, & Donnelly, 2002). Resulting addictions can persist for years after the abuse ends (Golding, 1999) and can, in turn, damage a woman's ability to develop or sustain relationships with others. If she does not get appropriate assistance, substance abuse and addiction may also harm a woman's ability to work and to be a parent (Riger et al., 2002).

Not every victim experiences all of these harms. Each woman's experience is mediated by the specifics of her situation, including factors that predate the victimization (such as the extent of prior abuse and mental health difficulties), the nature of the violent experience itself (such as the severity, frequency, level of psychological abuse, and extent of the coercive control that accompanied the violence), and the social and cultural context of the experience (Briere & Jordan, 2004). Unsupportive responses from one's social network, for example, are particularly powerful predictors of a problematic recovery process (Andrews, Brewin, & Rose, 2003). A woman who is told by those she loves to stop complaining and make the best of a bad situation or that the abuse is her own fault because she fails to fulfill her partner's needs typically experiences an increased sense of distress, hopelessness, and powerlessness.

Valarie's story helps to illustrate the problem. She is 32 years old and has three children with her husband. When her husband punched her twice in the face because she had not laundered a shirt correctly, Valarie called the police, and they arrested him. Later, Valarie explained to her attorney that "the law is of no help" because of what happened after her husband was arrested. As her advocate explained,

> First, her sister-in-law, who had been living with them and helping to care for the children while [Valarie] was at work, was upset at Valarie for calling the police and left. Since her husband was the only other person who cared for the children while she worked, she was left with no childcare. Second, when she called in sick at work (because her face was swollen and bruised) her employer told her the next sick day would be her last [day] working with him. The next day she confided what happened over the phone to the home-care worker who helps with her eight-year old mentally retarded child. While the worker was sympathetic, she called back later and abruptly cancelled the next three home-care visits. Desperate, [Valarie] called her own mother for help with the children. Her mother told her that she couldn't help and that she should go back to her husband. Finally, Valarie realized that without her husband, without childcare and without a job she would be unable to pay for rent, food and all the other necessities for herself and her children. She did what any reasonable person would do under the circumstances: she begged her husband to come home and apologized for calling the police. (Brief for the National Network to End Domestic Violence, 2006, Appendix B, pp. 56a–58a)

As of this writing, Valarie feels despairing, hopeless, and alone in the world (M. Merryman, personal communication, October 10, 2006). Just as social isolation is both a cause and an effect of victimization, conditions such as poverty and homelessness may do more than increase the likelihood of victimization; they also may exacerbate the impact of the violence once it occurs (Bassuk, Dawson, Perloff, & Weinreb, 2001; Bassuk, Melnick, & Browne, 1998). Indeed, the highest rates of PTSD can be found among women with the lowest incomes (Bachman & Saltzman, 1995; Greenfield et al., 1998; Vest, Catlin, Chen, & Brownson, 2002).

Impact on Employment

Domestic violence also affects a woman's ability to work. Studies show that survivors are more likely than others to miss days of work and to have been unemployed (Lloyd & Taluc, 1999). Research on low-income victims has shown that partner violence harms a woman's capacity to maintain work over time. Compared with low-income women who had not experienced partner violence, poor victims were one third as likely to maintain employment for at least 30 hours per week for 6 months or more during the year following the abuse, and they were only one fifth as likely to work full time during that period (Browne et al., 1999). One survivor, Bernice Hampton, described her options as follows: "I should fight for my life just to get to [my job at] Burger King? I don't think so. At the time, it didn't seem worth dying over" (Raphael, 2000, p. 16).

Abusive partners often play a direct role in undermining women's efforts to attain economic self-sufficiency by creating a wide range of obstacles to a victim's attempts to work or to go to school. These efforts include direct sabotage (e.g., destroying work, educational materials, or clothing), harassing women at their workplaces, refusing to provide transportation or child care, or inflicting visible bruises the night before a critical job interview (Bybee & Sullivan, 2005; Raphael, 2000).

For example, Bernice Hampton was 15 weeks away from graduating from licensed practical nurse training. She had been offered a job for after graduation and had just one class left to finish. The weekend before her last final exam, her partner took her books from her and refused to watch their children so that she could study. In the middle of the night before the exam, he raped her. She failed the test and was dropped from the program (Raphael, 2000).

Even in the absence of such interference, obtaining steady employment may prove difficult for domestic violence victims. Finding a job and securing reliable child care can be challenging for any woman, and women with little education and work experience often have access only to low-wage, unstable jobs that do not offer health insurance or flexible schedules. For women simultaneously contending with the psychological difficulties wrought by abuse and the threat of continuing violence, this may be an impossible situation to manage (Browne et al., 1999).

Impact on Children

Inevitably, the damage caused by domestic violence radiates out to other members of the family, especially to the children who often witness it (Holden, Geffner, & Jouriles, 2000). This starts early: National surveys have reported that 1 out of 6 obstetrics patients are battered (Gelles, 1988). Pregnant victims have an inflated risk of preterm labor, infection, miscarriage, and fetal or neonatal death (Curry, Perrin, & Wall, 1998; Parker, McFarlane, & Soeken, 1994).

The harm continues after birth. Approximately 20% to 25% of all children witness incidents of violence between their parents (L. A. McCloskey, Figueredo, & Koss, 1995; L. A. McCloskey & Walker, 2000; M. J. R. O'Brien, John, Margolin, & Erel, 1994), and 63% of these young people fare less well than other children on a wide range of behavioral, social, and academic measures. For example, although some children are quite resilient, many young witnesses to domestic violence become unable to control or express their own emotions and exhibit a strong tendency to blame themselves for what they have seen. School-age children, in particular, tend to react with withdrawal, depression, anxiety, or aggression (Kitzmann, Gaylord, Holt, & Kenny, 2003). The younger the child, the more severe the impact of witnessing adult-on-adult violence. When children are exposed to partner abuse just as they are developing initial belief systems about the world, about safety, and about caregivers, it can damage their core sense of self and of others (Chemtob & Carlson, 2004; Margolin, 2005; Wolfe, Crooks, Lee, McIntyre-Smith, & Jaffe, 2003). Later on, boys who witness violence between their parents demonstrate higher rates of bullying others, psychiatric emergency room visits, alcohol and drug abuse, juvenile court appearances, and suicide (Baldry, 2003; M. E. Evans & Boothroyd, 2002; Shumaker & Prinz, 2000; Women and Violence, 1990).

A child who enters a domestic violence shelter with his or her caretaker can be traumatized by the move itself as well as by the chaos of shelter life (Fantuzzo & Lindquist, 1989). Children whose mothers choose to avoid the disruption and risk of a shelter may face other risks: The mothers may be charged with failure to protect or lose temporary or permanent custody if the children continue to be exposed to violence at home (Riger et al., 2002). One survivor recalled,

> After the children, there was [my partner's] added threat that he would follow through with social services and have the children taken from me, as on some occasions I had fought back with the abuse—I have never understood this one either—what would the law have you do instead while someone is strangling you, throwing you up or down . . . flights of stairs, or slamming you in the back with a 2 × 4 board? (Brief for the National Network to End Domestic Violence, 2006, Appendix B, pp. 65a–68a)

The intergenerational impact is dramatically illustrated by a study of female homicides in New York City, which found that in 42% of such murders in which a second victim was also killed, that person was a child. In an additional 9% of cases, a child witnessed the murder, discovered the body, or was home when the crime occurred (Wilt, Illman, & Brody Field, 1995).

The impact of witnessing intimate partner violence on children does not stop when they mature; it can influence the degree to which an adult responds to provocation with words or with violence. Children who are raised watching one parent abuse the other may well follow suit; boys who witness violence against their mothers are more likely than others to batter female partners when they reach adulthood (Hotaling & Sugarman, 1986; Stith et al., 2000). Girls who witness violence against their mothers are far more likely to become victims of partner violence (Mitchell & Finkelhor, 2001). This unintentional home-schooling process also forges a link between domestic and stranger violence (Greenwald, 2002). Young people who witness domestic violence are, for example, more likely than others to commit sexual assault and engage in other forms of violence against strangers (Spaccarelli, Sandler, & Roosa, 1994; Wolfe, Wekerle, Reitzel, & Gough, 1995).

Impact on Extended Family

Finally, the impact of partner violence often extends to victims' extended family and friends. Victims of abuse are likely to be dependent on their partners for money, health care, child care, transportation, or housing (M. Bell & Goodman, 2001; Epstein, Bell, & Goodman, 2003). When they take overt steps to address the violence, they run the risk that their partner will cut off their financial support, remove them or their children from the partner's health care policy, or refuse to help in other ways (Butts Stahly, 1999). Even when under a court order to provide spousal or child support, many batterers refuse to make payments or delay doing so for long periods of time (Epstein et al., 2003). Other perpetrators refuse to assist with child care or to provide access to transportation. Still others force their victims to move out of the house or apartment they share, leaving the victims homeless (Barnett, 2001; Rose, Campbell, & Kub, 2000). Such actions are especially likely if the relationship ends.

In the face of these challenges, many domestic violence victims turn to those closest to them for a wide range of support, including emotional sustenance and material assistance (Goodkind, Gillum, Bybee, & Sullivan, 2003; Kocot & Goodman, 2003). Many women who escape from an abusive home, for example, cannot afford to stop working to take care of their children full time and must rely on family members for occasional babysitting or even temporary custody (Riger et al., 2002). A battered woman may need to move in with family or friends while she establishes herself educationally or financially (Riger et al., 2002). Although some victims are reluctant to seek such support (e.g., Barnett, Martinez, & Keyson, 1996; Dunham & Senn, 2000), and others have no such option (Kocot & Goodman, 2003), those who succeed in doing so experience fewer mental health problems (Carlson, McNutt, Choi, & Rose, 2002; Kocot & Goodman, 2003; Tan, Basta, Sullivan, & Davidson, 1995) and greater levels of safety over time (Goodman, Dutton, Vankos, & Weinfurt, 2005; Sullivan & Bybee, 1999).

A woman's family members and friends may be threatened with, or actually subjected to, violence and other forms of abuse by a batterer (Browne, 1987; Riger et al., 2002). If the abuser is successful in intimidating her family and friends, these threats will prevent the victim from seeking and obtaining support from key people in her life, forcing her to cope with the abuse alone (Riger et al., 2002). The story of one victim provides an example:

My father is a well-respected physician. People know him as a kind and generous man, and his patients love him. The man we knew at home though, was someone else entirely. My father emotionally abused my mother, myself and my siblings for as long as I can remember. He knows (and I say knows because the abuse continues to this day) that physically harming someone is against the law, therefore he has always been careful to keep his abuse to the more intangible realm of emotional and verbal violence and degradation. Until I left home for college, I lived in constant fear of my father. He would consistently go into rages that would last days because one of us had committed some minor "offense"—such as not kissing him goodnight, or loading the dishwasher incorrectly, or not saying our prayers properly. In his rages he would scream at us at the top of his lungs, yelling that we were worthless and ungrateful. He would call us all manner of filthy names, or stand with all his bulk—he's 6'4" and almost 300 lbs—right over us, or with his face shoved up in ours and yell, threatening to hit us. He would threaten to kill our mother, then sometimes he would taunt us, daring us to call the police. Of course we never called. My mother, who tried to protect us and therefore suffered the worst of the abuse, was afraid for her and our lives. She was sure that he would kill us if she tried to leave, or if she sought help. I remember begging her to leave him when I was little, and her explaining that she was too afraid of what he might do. She was afraid that if it came to court no one would believe us because we weren't black and blue. Reading other survivors' stories though, I realize that maybe no one would have believed us even if we were black and blue. (Brief for the National Network to End Domestic Violence, 2006, 72a–74a)

The physical, psychological, and economic consequences of partner violence for individual women and their families have led the CDC to estimate that such violence costs the nation in excess of $5.8 billion per year (National Center for Injury Control and Prevention, 2003). These costs are attributable to the direct consequences of domestic violence, including the medical and mental health care needs of victims ($4.1 billion) as well as lost productivity both during and after victimization ($1.8 billion).

However, they do not even begin to account for the enormous costs incurred by the civil and criminal justice systems in responding to intimate partner violence. Further, domestic violence is a major contributing factor to a range of other social ills such as child abuse and neglect, poverty, drug abuse, and homelessness.

Early and effective intervention in intimate partner violence cases could substantially reduce violence in the home, in the streets, and in future generations. Subsequent chapters address the questions of how far our society has progressed toward this goal and where we should go from here.

2

The Advocacy Response

Despite the overwhelming scope and devastating effects of domestic violence, until the start of the battered women's movement in the late 1960s neither the federal nor state governments made any real effort to alleviate the problem. In fact, the United States has had a long history of complicity in—and even approval of—intimate abuse, particularly when perpetrated by men against their wives and children. This approach had its roots in medieval Europe where wives were legally considered their husbands' chattel, and a disobedient woman risked public punishment (O'Faolain & Martines, 1974/1979). In the words of 13th-century French legal commentator Philippe de Beaumanoir (c. 1283/1992), "The husband should punish and correct his wife . . . in any way he sees fit (excepting where it causes loss of life or limb)" (p. 595). From the early colonial period onward, American courts followed British law by affirming the husband's right of "domestic chastisement." In the words of the Mississippi Supreme Court, this rule allowed a husband to "use salutary restraints in every case of a wife's misbehavior, without being subjected to vexatious prosecutions resulting in the mutual discredit and shame of all parties concerned" (*Bradley v. State*, 1824).

It was not until the late 19th century that the states finally abandoned the explicit endorsement of a husband's use of physical force to discipline his wife. In its place, courts adopted a family privacy theory: The legal system should avoid intervention in domestic violence cases out of a respect for the sanctity of the family and the intimacy of family relationships. As late as 1874, for example, the North Carolina Supreme Court stated, "If no *permanent* injury has been inflicted, nor malice, cruelty nor *dangerous* violence shown by the husband, it is better to draw the curtain, shut out the public gaze, and leave the parties to forget and forgive" (italics added; *State v. Oliver*, 1874). The family privacy theory predominated in most states well into the 20th century.

This shift in the rhetoric and rules applied to intimate abuse represented a gain for married women in abstract terms of dignity and status. After all, the government no longer affirmatively endorsed a husband's right to physical abuse. However, the family privacy theory had an insidious result: Because the new paradigm was more rational in its terms, it was less socially controversial and therefore harder to challenge. The bottom line for women, however, remained the same: If the courts refused to get involved, husbands could still beat their wives with little fear of state intervention or punishment.

In the medical and mental health communities, intimate partner violence was barely on the radar screen prior to the 1970s. Those few women who did seek help from medical providers rarely revealed the sources of their injuries, and physicians rarely asked questions. Health care providers who did learn about partner violence often advised women to solve the problem by working harder on their marriages. Others suggested that women leave their partners but failed to explore the potential obstacles to doing so (Dobash & Dobash, 1979).

At the same time, many mental health clinicians suggested that the client provoked the abuse to fulfill her own unconscious, presumably pathological needs (Snell, Rosenwald, & Robey, 1964). Others medicated their clients to alleviate their "stress," and many urged marital counseling, emphasizing the importance of maintaining family stability despite the violence (Danis, 2006; Dobash & Dobash, 1979). All of these themes echoed the one adopted by the justice system: Intimate partner violence is a private family matter, and intervention should be avoided if at all possible. It was from this context that the anti–domestic violence movement arose in the late 1960s and early 1970s.

THE EARLY DAYS OF THE ANTI–DOMESTIC VIOLENCE MOVEMENT

The anti–domestic violence movement grew out of the broader feminist movement of the late 1960s. This movement, in turn, was deeply influenced by the ongoing civil rights and antiwar movements, which framed African American peoples' struggles and opposition to the war in Vietnam in political terms (S. Evans, 1979; Freeman, 1975; Schechter, 1982).

One of the most common methodologies of the feminist movement was the *consciousness-raising group*. In these small groups, women had the opportunity to talk freely about their lives and to compare their experiences with those of other women. They learned that many problems they had thought were individual and shameful were actually widely shared. Through this process, they also uncovered the influence of previously unrecognized societal forces that shaped their roles and limited their opportunities (Freeman, 1975; Herman, 1992).

One of the most alarming discoveries made by women in consciousness-raising groups was that many of them had secretly suffered abuse at the hands of their intimate partners (Schechter, 1982). Women learned that such physical and sexual abuse was common, that official responses to survivors were woefully inadequate or even harmful and revictimizing, and that the public was shockingly ignorant about all of it. As women learned that they were not alone in enduring violence at home and that responsibility lay at least in part with the larger society rather than with them as individuals, they felt an enormous sense of relief, connection, and healing (Koss et al., 1994; Schechter, 1982).

Consciousness-raising group discussions spread across the country, and women began to develop a shared understanding of intimate partner violence as far more complex than a series of physical assaults perpetrated by aberrant men. In keeping with their newfound realization that many problems affecting women that had seemed personal were actually political in nature (Freeman, 1975; Herman, 1992), they came to understand the problem of intimate partner violence as an integral aspect of our society's systematic subordination of women. As legal scholar Elizabeth Schneider (2000) explained,

The battered women's movement defined battering within the larger framework of gender subordination. Domestic violence was linked to women's inferior position within the family, discrimination within the workplace, wage inequality, lack of educational opportunities, the absence of social supports for mothering, and the lack of child care. (p. 23)

Activists made clear connections between men's ability to succeed in violent exploitation and, among other things, women's social and economic inequality (Pagelow, 1984; Schechter, 1982). They reasoned that as long as women lacked equal pay, wealth, and job opportunities and were automatically assigned the role of primary caretaker of children, they would remain vulnerable to abuse (D. Martin, 1976; Pagelow, 1984).

The emerging view that domestic violence is a political rather than a personal problem led to an explosion of literature across numerous disciplines pointing to male privilege as the root cause of violence against women (Tjaden, 2004). Works such as Susan Brownmiller's (1975) *Against Our Will: Men, Women, and Rape*; Del Martin's (1976) *Battered Wives*; and Sandra Butler's (1978) *Conspiracy of Silence: The Trauma of Incest* made a persuasive case that violence against women was the inevitable result of the pervasive societal belief that men are entitled to control "their" women. This understanding was buttressed by the first large-scale study of family violence, which in 1980 demonstrated that partner violence was far more prevalent than previously understood (Straus, Gelles, & Steinmetz, 1980; see chap. 1, this volume).

As the pervasive scope of the problem became clearer, a broad social consensus grew around the idea that domestic violence could no longer be dismissed as a private matter even though it typically takes place at home behind closed doors. Activists now understood that because the problem was rooted in social and economic inequality, it could be solved only through societal reform. Grassroots organizers seized the moment and began to advocate for broader social change, and battered women began to seek out newly created services in ever-increasing numbers.

Early domestic violence activists who formulated a social change agenda focused on three urgent tasks: (a) securing shelter and support for battered women, (b) raising the nation's awareness of the problem, and (c) designing legal protections specially tailored to promote women's safety. On the basis of the view that domestic violence is a result of social and economic inequality rather than individual psychopathology, activists emphasized political and social advocacy for battered women instead of psychological treatment (Peled & Edleson, 1994). Advocates worked in part at a broad systemic level to improve institutional responses such as the criminal justice system. They also focused on the individual level, working with or on behalf of women to ensure access to resources such as housing, financial assistance, and child care.

Over the first few decades of the anti–domestic violence movement, advocates made astonishingly rapid progress in expanding the private and government resources available to abuse survivors. By 1976, grassroots anti–domestic violence organizers had established the first hotline in St. Paul, Minnesota, and the first shelter in Pasadena, California (Schechter, 1982). By 1978, advocates had established the National Coalition Against Domestic Violence (NCADV), an organization that became the national voice of the battered women's movement. In 1980, the NCADV sponsored the First National Day of Unity to mourn battered women who had died at the hands of a violent partner, to celebrate those who had survived, and to honor those who had worked to defeat abuse. All of these efforts helped to raise public awareness and to expand the supportive community available for battered women.

In 1984, the U.S. Attorney General established a Task Force on Family Violence to examine the scope and nature of the problem. By 1993, every state had adopted a protection order statute that authorized judges to award battered women essential forms of protection (C. Klein & Orloff, 1993). In 1985, Tracey Thurman became the first battered woman to sue a city for the police department's failure to protect her from her husband's violence. Thurman was partially paralyzed from being repeatedly stabbed and kicked in the head by her husband while police officers watched and did nothing. She won a $2 million judgment against Torrington, Connecticut, and her case served as a catalyst for police reform efforts nationwide. That same year, the Office of the U.S. Surgeon General issued a report that identified domestic violence as a major health problem. A resounding call to action, the report characterized the problem of partner violence as follows:

> That intimate nuclear family unit which broke bread together at dusk and which huddled close to hearth and home forms a rich part of the national lore and folk imagery. But the American family has also had its darker side, which has rarely turned public. As we are finding increasingly, the family united in common purpose and objective is frequently more a myth than a reality. Domestic life is often rent from within, making enemies of intimates. Domestic tranquility is, as we are becoming more aware, threatened profoundly by its internal dissentions, disruptions, and injurious and deadly conflicts. (Office of the U.S. Surgeon General, 1986, p. 12)

By 1982, 6 years after the first U.S. shelter opened its doors, estimates placed the number of shelters and safe home projects somewhere between 300 and 700 (Schechter, 1982), and NCADV had established the first national toll-free domestic violence hotline. The United States had moved from an era where no term for intimate abuse existed in the national lexicon to one of substantial public awareness of the problem, a growing perception that such abuse is unacceptable, and increasing political will to intervene.

At the individual level, activists also took a distinctly feminist approach, focusing on women's empowerment (Dutton, 1992; Schechter, 1982). Transition House, one of the first shelters for battered women, described its goals for a client this way:

> First of all, she gains a political awareness by viewing her own suffering for the first time in a social and political framework. And secondly, she discovers that the most effective way to confront the entire social, political, and economic system whose expressed interests are to keep the family with all its trappings of male supremacy and male privilege intact at her expense is to join together with other women and address the issues in a political way. (quoted in Schechter, 1982, p. 66)

Advocacy work was based on the premise that survivors needed the information, resources, and support to become safe; a political education to view intimate partner violence as a societal rather than an individual issue; and an opportunity to experience respect, validation, and self-determination. Advocates provided settings in which battered women, previously silenced, could share their stories. They sought to facilitate a woman's ability to make her own decisions, providing assistance only insofar as it supported her own way of organizing her life. Advocates carefully avoided imposing predetermined criteria for success or timetables for change on survivors (Bonisteel & Green, 2005). In shelters, support groups, hotlines, and courtrooms, advocates focused on the specific needs of individual women, helping them to articulate their goals, support each other, and achieve greater economic stability.

Consistent with this feminist orientation, the organizations that emerged from the early days of the battered women's movement were structured to empower their staff members as well as the battered women seeking their help. Throughout the 1960s and 1970s, numerous feminist organizations were committed to decentralized nonhierarchical power structures that included consensual decision making, job rotation and sharing, and equal salary distribution (Thomas, 1999). Shelters, for example, were envisioned as places of empowerment for both staff and residents. Battered women were encouraged to join shelter staff based on the experience they had to offer rather than on their level of professional expertise (Rodriguez, 1988). In her eloquent historical account of the movement, Susan Schechter (1982) described the dedication and commitment of early domestic violence advocates working together to establish a distinctly feminist process:

> The women's liberation movement not only helped create an atmosphere where women could understand and speak about battering; it also influenced the organization of work in the battered women's movement. Because male domination often inhibited women from talking and taught them to doubt their abilities, the women's liberation movement emphasized egalitarian and participatory organizational models. Consensus decision-making became an important political tool for some groups and organizations. . . . As a result of the abuse of power experienced in male dominated organizations, the women's liberation movement developed a strong suspicion of hier-

archy and leadership. . . . Egalitarian forms of working gave strength
to the battered women's movement. (p. 33)

PARTNERING WITH THE STATE
AND ERODING FEMINIST ORIENTATION

Early grassroots organizers sought complete independence from governmental institutions. The long history of the state's complicity in domestic
violence led the organizers to view government authority with suspicion,
seeing it as a major part of the problem rather than a source for solutions.
They rejected public funding on the ground that it might result in pressure to create organizational hierarchies counter to their preferred egalitarian and consensus-based models (Ahrens, 1980; Pennell & Francis,
2005).

However, as the movement successfully illuminated the scope of
domestic violence, it became clear that the problem was far too serious and
widespread to be resolved solely in the private realm. Shelter workers were
overwhelmed by an ever-increasing demand for space, and the resources
they could offer were inadequate to meet women's needs (Bonisteel &
Green, 2005). Some activists began to believe that the movement would not
achieve full political legitimacy in the absence of government sponsorship.
They also felt strongly that the state needed to take responsibility for a
problem of such massive proportions. Reluctantly, activists began to look
to the state for financial assistance as well as for legal and programmatic
interventions (Pennell & Francis, 2005; Pleck, 1987). Although this partnership with the government greatly expanded available resources, it also
diminished the movement's original feminist orientation.

An initial step on this path occurred in 1984, when intense grassroots
lobbying efforts culminated in the federal Family Violence Prevention and
Services Act (1984).[1] The legislation earmarked federal funding for programs serving victims of domestic violence. The act was a precursor to the
farther-reaching Violence Against Women Act of 1994 (VAWA). The

---

[1] Until this time, domestic violence remained a state rather than a federal issue, as is traditional with legislation related to family matters.

passage of VAWA reflected anti–domestic violence activists' enormous progress from a grassroots feminist campaign to a mainstream political movement (Haaken & Yragui, 2003). VAWA, which was enacted with broad bipartisan support, greatly expanded funding for victim services, research, and criminal justice reform. The statute was expanded in 2000 to provide battered immigrant women the opportunity to petition for naturalization as well as (among other things) to reauthorize grants to facilitate protection order enforcement, to limit the effects of domestic violence on children, to develop educational programs on woman abuse, and to add dating violence to the list of prohibited crimes against women (Victims of Trafficking and Violence Protection Act, 2000). The statute was authorized again in 2005 to expand support for prevention programs, to address the dating and sexual violence that teens experience, to more effectively address partner violence in Native American communities, to respond to survivors' needs for more transitional and permanent housing options, and to outlaw discrimination against survivors in public housing and much federally subsidized housing (Violence Against Women and Department of Justice Reauthorization Act, 2005).

Meanwhile, activists began pushing hard for greater responsiveness within the criminal justice system in an effort to increase women's access to its power and to send a clear social message that the state would no longer condone any violence against women. Such efforts focused heavily on mandatory arrest laws and no-drop prosecution policies. These transformations were heralded by many as a way to equalize the state's response to domestic violence with its traditional response to stranger-on-stranger violence (see chap. 4, this volume).

As activists tried to convince government officials to partner with them in these reform efforts, they made a strategic decision to fight a deeply entrenched class myth: that domestic violence was primarily perpetrated by poor men, who were seen as excessively violent by nature (Gordon, 1988; Pleck, 1987). Advocates knew this misconception had contributed to policymakers' lack of interest in partner abuse, had inhibited awareness of the actual scope of the problem, and had hindered women's ability to identify their own abusive situations—"I didn't think this happened to people like me!"

Early activists prioritized the message that partner violence is an issue affecting all women and that it crosses all socioeconomic and racial lines. As scholar Joan Meier (1997) explained,

> This was not merely a political tactic; it was also an expression of the fundamental creed of the battered women's movement that battering is culturally condoned, taught, and inherited, and that only fundamental social and cultural transformation in views of gender roles would put an end to it. (pp. 223–224)

The strategy served the movement well in many ways, contributing to a heightened awareness of violence against women in a variety of settings, including health care, religious institutions, suburban as well as urban areas, the employment sector, and college campuses (Richie, 2005).

The activist decision to join forces with the state had immediately obvious advantages. The number of programs that served victims of intimate partner violence increased by more than 50% between 1986 and 1994 (though they increased only 2% between 1994 and 2000; Farmer & Tiefenthaler, 2003). The types of services available also expanded significantly. Where earlier services had been essentially limited to small localized hotlines and shelters, in the 1980s, medical and legal professionals as well as community organizations developed nationally organized responses (Chalk & King, 1998). These expansions were made possible in part by an enormous increase in available funding from the government and mainstream private foundations.

However, the continued pressure for service expansion, combined with the strategic disregard of the role of poverty in domestic violence, new demands from government, and more mainstream funding sources, dramatically changed the movement's original, feminist focus on individual empowerment and shared power within organizations (Thomas, 1999). Domestic violence service providers faced increasing pressure to: (a) distance themselves from the organized antipoverty movement; (b) develop conventional, hierarchical organizational structures and hire traditionally credentialed staff; (c) specialize so that services fit with the limited mission of the agencies of which they were a part; (d) focus on measurable "outcomes" that were often distinct from the stated personal needs of individual survivors; and (e) develop clear criteria that limited the range of victims eligible to gain shelter entry.

Separation From Antipoverty Activists

The relentless, strategic emphasis on the classlessness of domestic violence was consistent with the reality that much of the early feminist theory was developed by White, heterosexual, middle-class women; their insistence on the centrality of gender as an organizing framework led to the marginalization of other formative aspects of identity, such as class, race, and sexual orientation (Bartky, 1997; Russo & Vaz, 2001). Many feminists viewed differences among women as quantitative rather than qualitative; an individual woman might be more or less oppressed than any other, but her experiences were not seen as substantively different. For many years, it was considered heresy to note any connections among race, class, and domestic violence (Schechter, 1982; Straus et al., 1980). As critical race theorist Crenshaw (1991) observed,

> There is . . . a thin line between debunking the stereotypical beliefs that only poor or minority women are battered, and pushing them aside to focus on victims for whom mainstream politicians and media are more likely to express concern. (p. 105)

The disconnection between the domestic violence and antipoverty movements was exacerbated by what Joan Meier (1997) called "a fundamental clash of ideologies and philosophies":

> The moral righteousness of the battered women's movement, which casts battering men as guilty perpetrators and battered women as innocent victims, sits uneasily with the poverty activists who see talk of moral judgment as a form of blaming the victim; at the same time, poverty progressives' emphasis on poverty as the cause of violent behavior in the family seems on the surface to be incompatible with the battered women's movement's emphasis on unjust gender oppression as the source and ultimate cause of domestic violence. (p. 223)

Until recently, there has been little, if any, scholarly investigation of poverty's role in battering (Ptacek, 1999). Even now, few of the services offered to victims focus on helping them achieve long-term economic independence, and services for victims of partner violence are much more likely to be available in affluent areas than in impoverished ones (Farmer & Tiefenthaler, 2003; Lott & Bullock, 2007; Tiefenthaler, Farmer, & Sambira, 2005). This lack of attention has done a grave disservice to battered women. Today, a large body of evidence suggests that poverty functions as a central contributing factor to the occurrence of domestic violence and severely curtails battered women's options for safety and escape.

Increased Hierarchy and Professionalization

As domestic violence programs grew in number and size, their staff members felt the need to create more hierarchical organizational structures both to manage themselves and, often, to appeal to the more conventional expectations of their funders (Schechter, 1982). Although hierarchies had numerous advantages in terms of efficiency and accountability, these structural changes had unforeseen repercussions. As one anonymous shelter staff member put it,

> We desperately need money and need to institutionalize. United Way criteria, however, mean having a board that sets policies, a director who directs, and salaries based on title, not need. We have never operated that way. Staff resents that salaries and policies will be determined by the board. . . . Staff is furious about losing control. . . . It's ironic that we've never been on more solid ground financially and more unhappy. I can't sleep at night. The board is pushing me one way and raising lots of money, and the staff is pushing me in another. (quoted in Schechter, 1982, p. 95)

Front-line staff members were less likely to be selected for leadership roles than before: They felt a diminished sense of stake in the organization as a whole, and many believed that hierarchical structures were antithetical to a movement designed to fight patterns of dominance and control in relationships (Schechter, 1982).

At the same time, donors pressured these organizations to change their hiring standards. Many new movement funders, both public and private, came from a more traditional perspective. They strongly preferred professional service provision over grassroots organizing or social change work. In some states, funding agencies required that a social worker with a master's degree supervise all paid staff (Schechter, 1982). Many domestic violence programs, desperate to retain the funding that had finally provided some degree of stability, submitted to these expectations and began to hire social workers and lawyers rather than community organizers (Bonisteel & Green, 2005). This new infusion of professionals expanded agency capacity in areas such as psychotherapy, legal services, and employment counseling. However, the change had a considerable negative impact as well. As professional services became the chief offering of domestic violence organizations, political activism moved toward the periphery. A new focus on a woman's internal psychology as a key to change (see chap. 3, this volume) diminished the attention paid to male responsibility for violence: Battered women began to be approached as "clients" rather than as "sisters" in a struggle against gender subordination (Schechter, 1982; Schneider, 2000). As one advocate put it, "I don't feel we are part of a movement to end violence against women any more. People are hired only to do specific jobs, not to be part of [something larger]" (quoted in Schechter, 1982, p. 95).

Overspecialization and Service-Defined Advocacy

With increased funding sources, advocacy programs for battered women proliferated in private and public settings, from shelters to prosecutors' offices to hospitals. However, this expansion changed the nature of the advocacy offered. As the field became increasingly fragmented, advocates often reluctantly focused less on holistic services designed to address the goals identified by the clients themselves and increasingly on specialized areas of assistance. Prosecutors' offices, for example, began to develop their own in-house advocacy services for battered women, with a focus on helping women pursue relief within the criminal justice system (Peled & Edleson, 1994). However, the work of these government advocates is limited by the fact that they are employed by, and therefore have an institutional loyalty to, the government. No matter how well they listen to a woman's story or work to meet her individually expressed needs, their primary task is to help her navigate the criminal justice system and cooperate in a "successful" prosecution for the state.

In their groundbreaking book, *Safety Planning With Battered Women*, Davies, Lyon, and Monti-Catania (1998) dubbed this new approach *service-defined advocacy*, in contrast with the *woman-defined advocacy* that had preceded it. In a service-defined approach, a woman is offered a limited menu of assistance based primarily on the availability of each item or on its consistency with the mission of the organization within which the advocacy services are embedded. Services are offered with little individualized attention to whether they promote a woman's personal sense of autonomy and self-esteem, fit into her particularized risk analysis or safety plan, or advance her plans for the future. By its very nature, a service-defined approach requires a woman to ignore critical aspects of her situation, such as economic dependency on the batterer, to focus on the narrow need that can be met by a particular provider (Smyth, Goodman, & Glenn, 2006). In contrast, a "woman-defined" approach gives a survivor the opportunity to collaborate meaningfully with an advocate in defining the forms of assistance she needs. As her situation changes or as her understanding of it shifts, she may change or refine her goals (Smyth et al., 2006).

Adopting a woman-defined or survivor-defined approach does not mean simply endorsing everything a victim says or wants. Instead, it means developing a relationship with a survivor through which the provider can come to understand and respect her perspective and the reasons underlying her choices. To do this, an advocate or provider must start from the assumption that a survivor is not making choices out of an inner masochism or other form of psychopathology but instead is arriving at a decision after weighing all of the relevant variables of which she is aware. An advocate's job may be to help a victim expand her thinking by adding new variables to the mix, by suggesting that she could accord different weight to certain variables, or by providing a new relationship (with the advocate her- or himself) that enables her to adopt a new approach to the weighing process. This perspective highlights and supports women's strength, autonomy, and control over their lives without ignoring the multiple factors limiting their range of choices (Burstow, 2003; Peled, Eisikovitz, Enosh, & Winstok, 2000). As legal scholar Elaine Chiu (2001) explained, a survivor-centered approach "recognizes the opportunities for action or decision while simultaneously recognizing the insurmountable obstacles that may prevent actions and decisions from reducing, eliminating or affecting the abuse" (p. 1258).

Compelling evidence exists that a survivor-defined as opposed to service-defined approach to advocacy not only empowers women but also promotes the fundamental goal of most advocates, psychologists, and justice system officials: ensuring a woman's physical safety (Bybee & Sullivan, 2002; Sullivan & Bybee, 1999). Using an experimental design—the gold standard in the field—researchers evaluated the long-term impact of a 10-week intensive advocacy intervention on the emotional well-being and safety of women leaving a domestic violence shelter in East Lansing, Michigan. The advocacy provided was survivor defined in that each advocate helped her client articulate her own personal needs and goals and then assisted her in obtaining corresponding community resources for herself and her children. Every 6 months for 2 years, researchers interviewed the partner violence survivors who participated in the program as well as members of a control group who did not receive the advocacy services. They found that women in the advocacy group reported less physical violence than did the women in the control group. In fact, over twice as many women in the advocacy group experienced no violence whatsoever during the 2-year period. These women also reported having a higher quality of life and perceived themselves as more effective in obtaining needed resources and interpersonal support. Finally, women in the advocacy group who wished to end their abusive relationships reported more success in doing so than those in the control group.

Increasingly Narrow Goals Set by Advocates

Consistent with this greater specialization and service definition, increased funding from private foundations and government grants created pressure on programs to demonstrate specific "results" in order to justify future contributions. In response to these incentives, providers began to emphasize concrete—but often less meaningful—conceptualizations of programmatic success. They maintained data on the percentage of program clients who were able to access additional services, leave their abusers, obtain a protection order, or find alternative shelter. Other important indicators, such as the degree to which women were able to gain control over their own lives, were no longer deemed as relevant (Schechter, 1982).

Although these measures undoubtedly captured important short-term improvements for many battered women, their growing dominance narrowed women's opportunities to collaborate with advocates to define success for themselves. In contrast to the earlier empowerment-based approach, in which advocates fostered a woman's determination of her own goals and schedule for change, strict outcome evaluation criteria presumed generic common goals and uniform trajectories (Smyth et al., 2006).

This tension continues to this day. A domestic violence victim who works with such a program must reshape her own personal goals and needs to fit into a narrow set of outcome criteria. If she is seeking commonly available and politically acceptable forms of assistance, such as shelter, job training, or court advocacy, her experience will be satisfactory. If instead, she envisions a life that is at odds with advocates' or funders' definitions of success, then she is far less likely to get meaningful help.

As one example, many survivors choose to remain in an abusive relationship. This may occur for a wide variety of reasons, including financial dependence, concern for children, a deep emotional connection, or fear of retributive violence (see chap. 5, this volume). However, one study showed that shelter workers felt more similar to and favored women who wished to leave their batterers (K. M. O'Brien & Murdock, 1993). Moreover, most shelter-based advocacy programs are located far from their clients' own neighborhoods and impose strict curfews in the belief that these measures will increase the safety of residents and staff members. An unintended consequence is that a resident finds herself in new community where she has no personal ties. As a result, her ability to remain connected to her partner or others in her social network is significantly undermined (Haaken & Yragui, 2003).

In many contemporary domestic violence advocacy programs, a woman's commitment to change is measured primarily by her willingness and ability to conform to the program's set expectations and priorities—even though this may be costly, risky, or out of step with her own goals (Smyth et al., 2006). The more vulnerable the woman, the more pronounced the power differential between her and the service provider may be, and the less likely it is that she will press for the provider to understand her particular situation (Smyth et al., 2006). This process can be profoundly disempowering (Smyth et al., 2006) and can lead victims to "resist" treatment or give up on the system altogether. As one executive director noted,

> If all that gets counted is whether a woman gets moved from homelessness to housing, and that kind of thing becomes a measure of good work, a program inevitably finds itself pushing a woman to pick the first housing she finds. That's especially true when affordable housing stock and rental vouchers in so many regions are in such short supply, and when there are time limits on shelter stays. But what if the first thing she finds is far away from public transportation, is in a new school district that will further disrupt her kids' lives, is a long commute from her job, and is far from the AA meetings that are beginning to be the source of her new community? Both the program and the woman are in a terrible position. But sometimes a "beggars can't be choosers mentality" drives funders, and the need to demonstrate simplistic "results" on annual performance reports pressures program staff, so they can't focus as fully on the way that stabilizing a woman's housing will have huge costs and will create instability in many other parts of her life. At the very least, we need to acknowledge these costs, both to the women we serve and to ourselves. Better yet, we need to challenge some of the cut-and-dried outcome measures that are being imposed on programs by funders and contractors and that prevent us from doing more meaningful work with women. (Katya Fels Smyth, personal communication, October 19, 2006)[2]

---

[2] Katya Fels Smyth is the founding executive director for On the Rise, an innovative program for homeless and precariously housed women in Cambridge, Massachusetts.

Narrow Shelter Eligibility Criteria
and Homogenizing Services

During this period, when shelter services became increasingly narrow and goal-oriented, the number of women who were seeking assistance continued to grow (Bonisteel & Green, 2005). Faced with a flood of victims seeking their services, shelter staff members were forced to prioritize some groups of women for admission over others. They began to develop criteria for assessing which clients were "appropriate" (Donnelly, Cook, & Wilson, 1999; Loseke, 1992; Rothenberg, 2003). Consistent with their outcome-oriented focus, many shelters deprioritized women with more complex needs, such as those with mental illness or drug and alcohol addictions (Grigsby & Hartman, 1997). Instead, they focused on women whom they perceived to be, on the whole, more responsive to available services (Donnelly, Cook, Van Ausdale, & Foley, 2005; Donnelly et al., 1999; Schechter, 1982). A woman had a far greater chance of admission if she was perceived by staff to be less likely to cause trouble, less likely to have retaliated against her abusive partner, and more likely to want to end her relationship with the abusive partner (Donnelly et al., 1999; Loseke, 1992; O'Brien & Murdock, 1993).

Over time, shelter workers—predominantly young, straight, and White—tended to replicate themselves in their client selection, and services were implicitly designed to meet the needs of this particular demographic (Donnelly et al., 1999). Even now, although women who do not fit this profile are not subject to overt discrimination, their different needs are less frequently considered in program design (Donnelly et al., 2005). Lesbian women, for example, may feel alienated by a shelter system in which staff members are at best poorly trained to work with them. Not only are they essentially forced to out themselves to explain their need for shelter services, they may worry that their abuser will be allowed into the all-women shelter space, or they may struggle with resident or even staff beliefs that women cannot truly hurt other women (Helfrich & Simpson, 2006; Simpson & Helfrich, 2005). Donnelly et al. (2005) conducted numerous interviews with shelter executive directors in Georgia and concluded that by not making allowances for the fact that not all women eat the same foods, worship the same deities, or discipline their children in the same ways, shelters marginalize women who do not adhere to the norm (i.e., women who do things differently from the White middle-class strategies employed by shelter staff). These women may feel that shelters are an inhospitable and foreign place, even as executive directors are protesting that they treat everyone equally. (p. 23)

Over time, shelters and other advocacy services for battered women became increasingly one size fits all (Donnelly et al., 1999). The importance of providing a variety of services to women with different ethnic and cultural backgrounds, different sexual orientations, and different vulnerabilities and needs has only recently begun to receive serious attention once again (see chap. 5, this volume).

CONCLUSION

The explosion of resources available to battered women starting in the late 1970s led to increased safety for thousands of survivors. However, this rapid growth, which was largely dependent on the new partnership advocates forged with the state, also resulted in the depoliticization, professionalization, and standardization of the anti–domestic violence movement. Today, most mental health and advocacy service providers have moved away from an explicitly feminist, survivor-defined approach to advocacy, in which a battered woman actively collaborates in framing the assistance she needs. These shifts have eroded the central notion of the early battered women's movement—that eradicating domestic violence depends on ending women's subordination and increasing their social and economic empowerment. Although current reforms represent a substantial improvement over the situation survivors faced 30 years ago, they also have operated to the detriment of many of the women the movement seeks to serve.

3

The Mental Health System Response

In the early days of the battered women's movement, services were provided almost exclusively through shelters or specialized domestic violence organizations (see chap. 2, this volume). Lay advocates provided mental health assistance rooted in feminist empowerment concepts, including 24-hour hotlines, short-term crisis counseling, support groups, and informational sessions (Lundy & Grossman, 2001). Efforts to help women cope with psychological and emotional distress tended to be political in nature, focusing on commonalities of the battering experience among women and the external societal forces that contribute to its occurrence. Counseling typically included helping women overcome the practical obstacles they faced in leaving their abusive partnerships, such as a lack of shelter, child care, and employment opportunities. Support for battered women was framed as collaboration among "sisters" in the fight against gender subordination.

Over time, increasing numbers of advocates with mental health training and professional degrees joined the ranks of shelter, agency, and hotline staff members. Despite the strong commitment to feminism and women's empowerment demonstrated by many of these professionals, they typically were trained to emphasize an internal, individual, psychological conception of intimate partner violence rather than an external, systemic, political one (Gondolf & Fisher, 1988). As a result, they brought with them substantially different ways of assisting victims. The psychological model focused on ways in which the trauma of abuse at the hands of an intimate partner creates psychological difficulties that in turn may inhibit a woman's ability to effectively protect herself (Rothenberg, 2003). Accordingly, mental health professionals responded primarily with internally focused psychotherapeutic solutions designed to help victims. Although many members of this newly professionalized generation of battered women's service providers shared the broader political perspective of lay advocates, their focus on mental health over practical assistance and social change had an unintended but profound impact on the movement: It cast battered women as clients with psychological difficulties rather than as victims of social oppression.

Early on, a tension arose between these two approaches to improving survivors' lives. Many lay advocates resisted the more psychological focus as apolitical and inappropriately medicalized (Chalk & King, 1998; Lundy & Grossman, 2001; Schechter, 1982). Although they believed that some of their clients could benefit from more intensive psychological counseling, they worried that this shift in emphasis would expose more battered women to the disempowering conceptions that the professional psychological community historically had held. For example, mental health professionals had explained victimization as the fulfillment of a battered woman's masochistic needs (Snell, Rosenwald, & Robey, 1964); promoted medication for victims, with a focus on symptom reduction rather than problem solving; and emphasized the importance of maintaining family stability no matter how great the costs (Dobash & Dobash, 1979). Although lay advocates understood that the new generation of mental health professionals who worked directly with abuse survivors held more progressive views than the generation that preceded them, they worried that their professional colleagues might unwittingly harm battered women: Would they recommend couples counseling without understanding the risk when partners have unequal access to power? Would they prescribe medication without links to other services? Would they expose women to the risk that diagnosed psychological "problems" would be used against them in child custody or child welfare proceedings (Warshaw & Moroney, 2002)? Lay advocates also feared that a focus on survivors' symptoms would substantially undermine activists' efforts to place partner violence in a broader political context and to obtain additional resources for battered women. As domestic violence researchers and activists Edward Gondolf and Ellen Fisher (1988) explained, "The abuse 'victim' has . . . become a new population to 'treat,' rather than [to] advocate for or empower" (p. 1).

Many mental health professionals, for their part, understood lay advocates' focus on external practical factors as a potentially effective long-term political strategy to garner attention and assistance in the fight against domestic violence. Their professional training, however, was rooted in a medical model that explained emotional distress as a product of individual pathology, and the reimbursement structure under which they operated required diagnoses and psychological treatment plans. Moreover, they knew that battered women were experiencing real individual psychological difficulties. As a result, when faced with a woman struggling with debilitating symptoms, they focused on providing immediate psychological help rather than on analyzing and challenging the problem's connection to larger issues of political oppression.

Today, both groups have come a long way toward understanding and appreciating the respective contributions of the predominantly political and the predominantly psychological perspectives on woman abuse. However, collaborative efforts across this divide remain scarce, limiting both groups' ability to respond to the complex realities of survivors' lives (Gomez & Yassen, 2007; Warshaw & Moroney, 2002). In addition, few theoretical models successfully integrate the two approaches.

Chapter 3 explores the ways in which, over the past 30 years, mental health theoreticians and practitioners have attempted to explain and respond to victims' experiences. It also analyzes the limitations of current mental health responses and the importance of integrating political and psychological perspectives, focusing on feminist therapy as one promising example.

EXPLANATORY THEORIES

For decades, mental health professionals have attempted to explain both the scope and the frequency of partner violence and why many victims stay with their abusive partners even after an assault.

Learned Helplessness and the Battered Woman Syndrome

In the 1960s and 1970s, many psychological researchers and theorists saw battered women as masochists who unconsciously enjoyed being abused and sometimes even provoked the batterer's actions (Schechter, 1982; Snell et al., 1964). For example, an article written by Snell et al. (1964) and published in the highly regarded *Archives of General Psychiatry* described the dynamics of intimate partner violence as follows: "The essential ingredient seems to us to be the need both husband and wife feel for periodic reversal of roles; she to be punished for her castrating activity; he to reestablish his masculine identity" (p. 111).

Over the next 10 years, psychological theories that attempted to explain intimate partner violence became less overtly misogynistic but nevertheless depicted domestic violence as caused by women victims. Abuse was considered either the result of a woman's provocation or the inevitable consequence of her demands for equality in an intimate relationship (Koss et al., 1994; Schechter, 1982). By the early 1980s, psychological theories of domestic violence had largely discarded these victim-blaming concepts. Professionals began to focus on battered women's mental health issues and behavior as a response to, rather than a cause of, the violence they endured.

Psychologist Lenore Walker pioneered much of this new thinking. According to her concept of the "battered woman syndrome," victims become trapped in abusive relationships through two processes: learned helplessness and the cycle of violence. On the basis first of anecdotal accounts (1979) and subsequently of formal interviews with hundreds of survivors (1984), Walker posited that women try to stop the abuse by changing their own behavior to appease the batterer. When they realize that their actions have no effect, they come to view their efforts at self-preservation as futile. These women "learn" to be helpless, a perspective that becomes generalized to other parts of their lives and can result in depression, overwhelming fear, low self-esteem, anxiety, and psychological paralysis.

Walker theorized that a victim's sense of helplessness is exacerbated by a three-stage cycle of violence perpetrated by the batterer. In the first *tension-building* stage, the abusive partner expresses anger and hostility without violence. The resulting tension gradually builds until, in the second stage, the *acute battering incident*, the batterer unleashes his aggression and becomes physically violent. In the third *loving contrition* stage, the batterer tries to make up for his abuse by apologizing, excusing his actions, proclaiming his love and loyalty, and trying to persuade his partner to stay with him. This cycle repeats, and coupled with battered women's psychological state of learned helplessness, it keeps women trapped with their abusive partners, feeling unable to change the situation and at the same time hopeful that the loving contrition stage will last. Walker's theory led her to argue that assertiveness training and psychotherapy are critical tools for helping battered women gain the self-esteem they need to survive abuse.

The profound influence of the battered woman syndrome lay in its ability to explain a woman's decision to remain in an abusive relationship in a way that evoked public sympathy. As sociologist Bess Rothenberg (2003) explained,

> Ultimately, the entire battered women's movement and its appeals to the public centered on effectively arguing that abused women do not stay with their partners by choice. Only by convincing the public of this claim were advocates able to justify the need for public interventions into the private lives of citizens. The initial success of the movement came to depend greatly on a discourse that emphasized the ways in which battered women were trapped in abusive relationships. (p. 774)

However, this new understanding of domestic violence was not without costs. Many criticized Walker for overemphasizing obstacles rooted in internal psychological difficulties and underemphasizing those stemming from external real-world powerlessness (Bonisteel & Green, 2005). Many battered women, for example, are unable to leave their abusive partners because of inadequate resources such as education, job training, employment, housing, child care, and financial and legal support (Goodman, Koss, & Russo, 1993). To be fair, Walker's writing makes clear that a victim's "sense" of helplessness is often more than a psychological dynamic and may include a realistic appraisal of her lack of options for achieving safety (e.g., Walker, 1979). Critics still charged that by failing to sufficiently emphasize these practical obstacles, Walker's theory might lead many to mistakenly blame a woman's inability to escape abuse on her own psychological helplessness. The depiction of battered women as psychologically paralyzed and passive in the face of violence could create a highly stigmatizing focus on survivors' personal pathology.

Battered Women as Survivors

In response to this critique, theorists and researchers have developed more nuanced views of women's responses to intimate partner violence. Each of these new approaches attempts to take into account both the psychological and structural realities of battered women's lives (Koss et al., 1994). For example, scholar–activists Edward Gondolf and Ellen Fisher (1988) conducted an empirical study of more than 6,000 battered women in Texas shelters; their research demonstrated the strength battered women display in the face of insufficient assistance from the government and civil society. According to Gondolf and Fisher's survivor hypothesis, women are stymied in their efforts to stay safe not primarily because of psychological obstacles but because of inadequate community support, including a dearth of domestic violence services, cultural and religious beliefs that prioritize the sanctity of marriage and family, and a lack of economic and social opportunities for poor and marginalized victims. Survivors' psychological difficulties matter but primarily because they interfere with their efforts to cope with externally imposed circumstances.

Additional studies support this view. Researchers have shown that most battered women are far from helpless; instead, they become increasingly active and persistent in their attempts to protect themselves as the abuse grows more frequent or severe (Goodman, Dutton, Weinfurt, & Cook, 2003; Lempert, 1996). Women's strategies are diverse and include learning to predict violent episodes; developing escape plans; placating their partners; fighting back; and seeking outside help from family, friends, police, clergy, mental health professionals, and domestic violence agencies (Goodman et al., 2003). The survivor hypothesis does not claim to be a comprehensive explanation of women's emotional responses to partner violence, but it encourages providers to address external obstacles to a victim's safety and well-being before addressing internal psychological issues.

Posttraumatic Stress Disorder
and Complex Posttraumatic Stress Disorder

In addition to exploring women's responses to abuse on a continuum from helplessness to strength, theoreticians sought a comprehensive explanation of the seemingly disparate emotional and psychological symptoms many victims experienced. Feminist activists and mental health professionals were among the first to recognize that these symptoms were similar to those observed in soldiers after combat. In both cases, a new diagnosis of posttraumatic stress disorder (PTSD) was developed to account for the full range of victims' experiences. As described in chapter 1 (this volume), PTSD symptoms include *intrusive symptoms* (reliving the traumatic experience as if it were continually recurring in the present, through nightmares and flashbacks), *avoidant symptoms* (emotional numbing, withdrawal, or the repression of memories of violent incidents), and *hyperarousal* (being in a constant state of alertness for and expectation of danger, which often leads to irritability and angry outbursts; Housekamp & Foy, 1991; Kemp, Green, Hovanitz, & Rawlings, 1995).

Energized by the idea that PTSD represents a bridge between the horrors of war and those of domestic life, advocates and therapists joined a growing veterans' movement to fight for the official recognition of PTSD as a diagnosis (Herman, 1992). As a direct result of their efforts, PTSD was added to the third edition of the American Psychiatric Association's *Diagnostic and Statistical Manual of Mental Disorders* (*DSM*; American Psychiatric Association, 1980), the "bible" of the psychiatric establishment.

Over the next decade, studies began to reveal an astonishingly high prevalence of PTSD among domestic violence survivors. One analysis of a large set of existing studies found that almost 64% of battered women displayed symptoms that could be diagnosed as PTSD (Golding, 1999). Other studies showed that approximately half of the women who experienced PTSD remained symptomatic even after they had been out of a violent relationship for 6 to 9 years (Woods, 2000). Researchers and service providers also found that PTSD was associated with other psychological difficulties, including substance abuse (Kilpatrick, Acierno, Resnick, Saunders, & Best, 1997), depression (Campbell, Sullivan, & Davidson, 1995), suicidality (Thompson, Kaslow, & Kingree, 2002), and anxiety (Kemp et al., 1995). By the early 1990s, PTSD had become the most commonly used framework for understanding women's psychological responses to domestic violence (Goodman et al., 1993).

Missing from the PTSD conceptualization, however, was an appreciation of the ways in which domestic violence is different from other acute forms of trauma. Unlike the experience of being assaulted by a stranger in combat, domestic violence victims experience repeated abuse, committed by someone they know and care about, often over a long period of time. Furthermore, at least in the case of intimate terrorism, the physical abuse is accompanied by ongoing intimidation, isolation, coercion, and humiliation. As a result, victims can feel—and actually be—abandoned by someone they thought they could trust and endangered in places they thought were safe (Koss et al., 1994). These feelings can lead to a tendency toward self-condemnation and a sense of disconnection from others that pervades all of a victim's relationships (Herman, 1992).

In the early 1990s, these distinctions led psychiatrist Judith Herman to propose a new diagnosis that she called *complex PTSD* (Herman, 1992).[1] This diagnosis acknowledges that for partner violence victims (as well as for survivors of other forms of chronic interpersonal abuse, particularly in childhood), trauma might be part of a victim's everyday life for a long period of time. As a result, victims of intimate abuse are more likely than other trauma survivors to struggle with overwhelming feelings of sadness, rage, anxiety, self-hatred, and profound distrust of others; to have self-destructive impulses; and to have trouble forming intimate relationships (Herman, 1992; van der Kolk et al., 2005). In Herman's words,

> People subjected to prolonged, repeated trauma develop an insidious, progressive form of post-traumatic stress disorder that invades

---

[1] This proposed diagnosis also is referred to as "disorder of extreme stress, not otherwise specified" (often denoted by the acronym DESNOS; van der Kolk, Roth, Pelcovitz, Sunday, & Spinazzola, 2005).

and erodes the personality. While the victim of a single acute trauma may feel after the event that she is "not herself," the victim of chronic trauma may feel herself to be changed irrevocably, or she may lose the sense that she has any self at all. (p. 86)

Although complex PTSD has not yet been accepted by the psychiatric establishment as an official diagnosis, it is nevertheless widely used to explain the complicated constellations of psychological and relational difficulties with which domestic violence victims often struggle (Roth, Newman, Pelcovitz, van der Kolk, & Mandel, 1997). The PTSD and complex PTSD diagnoses did much to destigmatize domestic violence victims by characterizing their sometimes counterintuitive behaviors (e.g., staying with their battering partners) as a result of externally inflicted psychological harms rather than internal psychological deficits. By putting battered women in the same category as combatants, they also facilitated a renewed focus on nonblaming social and professional support for survivors (Bonisteel & Green, 2005). However, despite these improvements, some feminist critics have pointed out that PTSD remains "by definition a disorder, with features that are characterized as symptoms" (Bonisteel & Green, 2005, p. 28), which in turn are perceived, within a psychiatric framework, as pathology. No matter how supportive and empathic the framework, these critics suggest imposition of an official diagnosis can pathologize survivors rather than help them develop a strength-based identity. A diagnosis tends to emphasize an individual's need to control herself rather than to gain power over real-world obstacles (Burstow, 2003). Although a great deal of controversy remains about whether a woman's responses to abuse should ever be labeled as a "disorder," most mental health professionals— even many feminist practitioners—find the concept of PTSD extremely useful in understanding battered women who seek their help.

MOVING FROM THEORY TO PRACTICE: MENTAL HEALTH MODELS ON THE GROUND

In practice, mental health professionals working in domestic violence agencies and mental health centers have at their disposal a variety of models to address survivors' trauma, including (but not limited to) *psycho-dynamic, psychoeducational,* and *cognitive–behavioral* approaches. Thera-pists often integrate several of these approaches in their work with particular clients, although some prefer to adhere closely to a single model (Abel, 2000; Lundy & Grossman, 2001). Put simply, psychodynamic ther-apy focuses on helping clients gain insight into underlying and possibly unconscious psychological conflicts that shape their response to abuse (Lundy & Grossman, 2001). Psychoeducational approaches focus on teaching clients coping strategies for dealing with the psychological con-sequences of domestic violence. Cognitive–behavioral interventions emphasize the ways in which trauma disrupts clients' positive beliefs about themselves and the world and help them replace maladaptive beliefs—that they are responsible for the abuse, that they deserved it, or that they are no longer safe anywhere—with more adaptive ones (Hem-bree & Foa, 2003; Kubany, Hill, & Owens, 2003; Resick & Schnicke, 1992). Recent research on psychological trauma has led providers using any of these approaches to be particularly alert for symptoms of PTSD in their clients and to emphasize them in their treatment (e.g., Kubany et al., 2003).

Each of these models has something valuable to offer to a woman cop-ing with abuse and its emotional consequences. None of them, however, incorporates into its core conceptual framework attention to the social conditions that cause and maintain domestic abuse and other forms of oppression in women's lives. This does not mean that practitioners who use these models are apolitical or value neutral. To the contrary, almost all take as a starting point the assumptions that a woman is entitled to safety regardless of her choice of partner, religion, or community and that she is not responsible for her partner's decision to batter her even if she is irritable, sullen, cruel, or provocative. But by failing to include a central focus on the societal conditions that facilitate domestic violence and the practical obstacles to battered women's safety, these models fail to address the full range of survivors' needs.

As many practitioners readily admit, treatment models must focus more attention on the major external challenges faced by so many domes-tic violence victims, including ongoing violence, economic dependence, homelessness, unemployment, and isolation from family and community. Although some providers believe that such an approach goes beyond the scope of mental health practice, others acknowledge that internal psychological and external situational difficulties are inextricably intertwined. Women's emotional well-being cannot be improved without integrated attention to their material and social conditions (Grigsby & Hartman, 1997; Smyth, Goodman, & Glenn, 2006). As theorists and practitioners Grigsby and Hartman (1997) explained,

> Most traditionally trained therapists have been taught to view all clients' struggles from an individualistic, not social, perspective. Asking therapists to recognize the barriers facing these women is asking [them] to recognize a daunting and overwhelming worldview. Yet this is precisely what is required to work effectively with this, and any, oppressed population. To continue to collude with an individual pathology framework is at best, ineffective and, at worst, detrimental to the welfare of clients from oppressed populations. (p. 486)

Feminist Therapy as a Bridge Between the Internal and External

Feminist therapy theory—a perspective that can infuse the practice of providers by using the traditional techniques described above—offers a set of principles that attempt to integrate the internal and external difficulties survivors face. Like the battered women's movement itself, feminist therapy theory grew out of consciousness-raising groups in the 1960s as a reaction to perceived sexism in traditional therapeutic models (M. Brabeck & Brown, 1997; Worrell & Remer, 1992). Inspired by these group conversations, therapists with a wide variety of theoretical orientations began to understand their work in political terms and to incorporate the perspective of feminist theory into their work (Ballou, Matsumoto, & Wagner, 2002; L. S. Brown, 1994). Despite the variety of techniques used, all feminist therapists locate the source of psychological problems squarely in a woman's external context and emphasize how a woman's social and material conditions influence her psychological status (L. S. Brown, 2004; Warshaw & Maroney, 2002).

Feminist therapists view domestic violence within a political context in which there are few obstacles preventing men (or those with more power) from using violence against women (or those with less power; Herman, 1992). As L. S. Brown (2004), an early feminist therapy theorist, wrote,

> Certain forms of trauma are viewed by feminist theory as represent-ing, at the individual or interpersonal level, the intended conse-quences of institutionalized forms of discrimination such as sexism, racism, classism, heterosexism, anti-Semitism and so on. When a husband beats his wife . . . a feminist therapist will view these experi-ences as not simply trauma but as trauma for which special vulnera-bilities were created by bias and unfair hierarchies of value in the culture. These forms of violation are seen as strategies for upholding an oppressive cultural status quo. (p. 465)

Specific approaches to treatment consistent with this overall perspec-tive vary widely across practitioners, but all emphasize a core set of prac-tices and principles aimed at exposing power disparities (L. S. Brown, 2004). In the domestic violence context, these include recognition of the ways in which social, cultural, and economic oppression influence women's emotional well-being; emphasis on understanding the subtle as well as the more apparent ways that abuse operates in a relationship; recognition of survivors' resistance and strength; a focus on a victim's immediate external material circumstances; and attention to the impor-tance of social support and community engagement.

The Role of Oppression

Feminist therapists maintain that a survivor's suffering is not only a direct consequence of the abuse itself but also is compounded by society's inad-equate and often unsupportive response. The problem is particularly pro-nounced for women from disempowered groups, including women of color; gay, bisexual, or transgendered women; poor women; immigrant women; and women with disabilities (L. S. Brown, 2004). In an effort to help a client see the structural causes of her emotional distress, a feminist therapist will both invite her to recognize how societal forces have shaped her self-awareness and remain open to learning about the client's particular experience. As feminist therapist and activist Janet Yassen explained,

> I bring the political into the room in very subtle and soft ways. For example, I might say "I hear about this kind of thing so often from so many women. I think it actually happens a lot. Did you know that? And what do you think about that?" Or I will tell a client, particularly if she is a new immigrant and unfamiliar with the laws of this country, that it is against the law to be hit. That is a political statement. (Janet Yassen, personal communication, December 18, 2006)[2]

It is not always easy to bring the issue of gender oppression into the room in a useful, nonjudgmental way. It requires patience, skill, and a clear sense of the importance of the task. As one feminist counselor explained,

> I have felt ambivalent talking to, for example, a poor Latina woman with few resources about the idea, developed by White, middle-class feminists, that domestic violence is in part a tactic to subordinate women. I worry that a lot of women don't resonate immediately with that way of thinking. But if you have time, and you earn a client's trust, then raising those issues with anyone in a culturally sensitive way can be very powerful, affirming, and explanatory. It can help her make sense of why this man is battering and why everyone seems to be supporting him. If she begins to understand the social and cultural underpinnings of the violence, the pragmatic outcome is that she can stop blaming herself, stop making excuses for the batterer, and start looking for solutions in new ways. It can shift her way of thinking and give her alternatives to the idea that she needs to change. (Susan Marine, personal communication, December 12, 2006)[3]

Feminist therapists also emphasize the role that other forms of oppression may play in a woman's life. A feminist therapist is likely to

---

[2] Janet Yassen is the crisis services coordinator at the Victims of Violence Program, a program of the Cambridge Health Alliance in Cambridge, Massachusetts. The program was cofounded by Mary Harvey and Judith Herman in 1984 and is recognized nationally and internationally for its work with trauma survivors.

[3] Susan Marine is currently director of the Harvard College Women's Center in Cambridge, Massachusetts. She is the former violence prevention coordinator for the City of Cambridge at the Cambridge Public Health Department and a counselor–advocate at Women's Information Services (WISE), in Lebanon, New Hampshire.

understand, for example, that a client newly arrived from Haiti may be silent and unforthcoming not because she is guarded, withholding, or treatment resistant but because she is worried that if she talks openly she may be deported or may inadvertently harm people who have helped her gain entry into the country illegally (Gomez & Yassen, 2007).

Knowledge of Abuse Dynamics

Many feminist therapists also educate themselves thoroughly about the interpersonal dynamics of abuse and the subtle and overt nature of coercion and control that is so often part of the picture. They learn to listen for these dynamics without imposing their own views on a client. As one practitioner noted,

> A feminist therapist needs to hear the client report with a therapeutic ear but also with an ear for reality—how people who batter insinuate their power in all kinds of domestic ways. So a feminist therapist would be really dogged about looking for issues of volition. What are the ways in which you are systematically yoked, without knowing it? The goal would be a therapeutic inquiry about the minutiae that reveal the whole. So the therapist would ask questions like "How did it get decided that he would be coming into your bed that night?" "How often does he call you like that?" "Do you ever turn off your cell phone?" "Are you allowed to turn off the cell phone?" Without the minutiae, you don't see patterns, threat, grooming, and build-up; so you wouldn't know where to intervene. It's this combination of macro and micro: Because you have this knowledge—a picture of what happens to battered women—you know how to get into the minutiae, the small and mute ways his power gets expressed. Because it is in those tiny ways that she can begin to wake up and chart a new path. (Robin Zachary, personal communication, December 20, 2006)[4]

A Focus on External Circumstances

In addition to raising consciousness about political realities and the dynamics of battering, feminist therapists often respond directly to a

---

[4] Robin Zachary is the group therapy coordinator at the Victims of Violence Program (see footnote 2 for a description).

woman's current life circumstances. If a woman is struggling with poverty or homelessness, for example, the fact that her children do not have a mattress to sleep on is considered relevant—even paramount—to the therapy (Harvey, 1996; Herman, 1992). Although any ethical therapist would consider the material circumstances of her client and might make a few phone calls to help a woman in such dire straits, feminist therapists make it their business to learn as much as they can about relevant social service systems and community resources, so that they know where their clients can get the help they need and what obstacles they may face in accessing these systems. They build alliances with key service providers, such as immigration attorneys, shelter staff, and housing advocates so that they can call and pave the way for a client who is ready to seek that kind of help. When a woman expresses deep mistrust of a particular institution—perhaps because she has had bad experiences in the past or comes from a country where social institutions are used as weapons against citizens—a feminist therapist might even accompany her client to an appointment. Not only does this serve a critical support function for the victim, but it also helps the therapist learn first hand what it takes for a client to ask for help from impersonal, complex, and intimidating agencies (Gomez & Yassen, 2007; Latta & Goodman, 2005). As feminist therapist Robin Zachary put it,

> When you as the therapist have the imprimatur of a respected and trusted person, you need to build on that to connect your client with others who can be helpful. When you know that you have been let into the inner sanctum—the client has finally taken you into her life and been real with you—you have the obligation to become a transition to a trusting relationship with other individuals and communities. If the circumstances warrant it, I will even take someone to get a restraining order, to an acupuncture appointment, to a nurse or doctor, to an AA meeting, to a shelter or a domestic violence agency. And while I am there, I will help her articulate things she has said to me but cannot express to others. (Robin Zachary, personal communication, December 20, 2006)

Importance of Resistance

Feminist therapists also help their clients understand the ways in which they already have resisted victimization or demonstrated strength and protested in the face of difficulty. Therapists may, for example, work with their clients to identify small private acts, such as refusing to cry in the face of a beating or secretly giving an abusive partner day-old coffee, that are in fact acts of defiance on which further resistance can be built (Wood & Roche, 2001). Eventually, the therapist may encourage a woman to engage in new forms of resistance as a step toward healing (Herman, 1992; Walker, 1994). Such protest may take a relatively private form, such as going back to school in the face of disapproval by a batterer and his family (L. S. Brown, 2004), or it may be more public—such as volunteering at a shelter or hotline; raising money for a domestic violence-related cause; or becoming involved in related issues such as fair housing, hunger, or child maltreatment.

Centrality of Social Support

Finally, feminist therapists often highlight the damage that stigma and isolation inflict on battered women's lives and help survivors recreate social ties that have been disrupted by an abusive partner. As Judith Herman (1992) explained,

> The core experiences of psychological trauma are disempowerment and disconnection from others. Recovery, therefore, is based upon the empowerment of the survivor and the creation of new connections. Recovery can take place only within the context of relationships; it cannot occur in isolation. (p. 133)

A feminist therapist may help a client repair or build new social ties by paying careful attention to the development of his or her own relationship with the client; helping the client find ways to connect with others in her religious, ethnic, or neighborhood communities; and encouraging her to join with others in social action. One feminist therapist described her own work to build support for her client as follows:

> If my client's friends and family have not been supportive or helpful to her, I will help her think about alternative communities—more progressive churches within the community or in a nearby neighborhood. "Are there people within the community who can be your ally? Who in your world can you turn to?" Or I might refer her to a group

that can stand for an alternative community of supportive people. Once my client can name a potential supporter, I may try to bring her into our work if I think that would be helpful. "Have your sister come in and we can talk about the safety plan with her." One client brought in her best friend. I welcomed her as a member of the client's inner circle. We talked about a plan for how to best respond if the husband contacted the friend. (Robin Zachary, personal communication, December 20, 2006)

Limitations of Feminist Therapy

Despite feminist therapy's relative success in merging an externally focused empowerment perspective with a recognition of internal psychological harm, this approach has its own limitations (Sharma, 2001). Perhaps most important, the emphasis on gender-based oppression has led some feminist therapists to neglect issues stemming from race, class, immigration status, ethnicity, sexual orientation, socioeconomic status, religion, and other aspects of a battered woman's identity (Green & Sanchez-Hucles, 1997; Grigsby & Hartman, 1997).

Furthermore, although numerous exceptions exist, feminist therapy remains for the most part a highly regulated process, in which the therapist meets the client in an office for a specified period at a regularly scheduled time. However, many marginalized women will not go to a therapy office for reasons ranging from the logistical (lack of transportation, child care, or insurance) to the cultural (shame, fear of the stigma associated with presumed mental illness, or unfamiliarity with therapy as an intervention) to the historical (anxiety stemming from past experiences with mental health-related institutions) to the interpersonal (fear of retaliation from the batterer; Cachelin & Striegel-Moore, 2006; Khamphakdy-Brown, Jones, Nilsson, Russell, & Klevens, 2006; Scheppers, van Dongen, Dekker, Geertzen, & Dekker, 2006). These women cannot benefit from therapy in an office setting, no matter how culturally sensitive the therapist.

Finally, although feminist therapists underscore the social isolation at the heart of many victims' experience and the resulting need to help victims reconnect with social networks, they could go much further in helping women reengage with others. For example, they might facilitate community conversations, lead groups in nontraditional settings such as hair salons and churches, or help women develop self-help projects in their own communities (Latta & Goodman, 2005; for a more in-depth discussion, see also chap. 6, this volume). Although social workers already engage in this kind of work, it is rare for other mental health professionals, such as psychologists and psychiatrists, to do so. If these therapists expanded their practices beyond more conventional forms of mental health intervention, they could substantially improve women's ability to move past experiences of abuse.

SYSTEMIC LIMITATIONS OF CURRENT MENTAL HEALTH PRACTICE

Despite the mental health system's substantial progress in assisting battered women, particularly through the adoption of feminist therapy principles, far more remains to be done. As described below, systemic challenges exist for practitioners of all models. First, the majority of mental health practitioners receive little or no training in domestic violence, hindering their ability to screen for and work with survivors. Second, in the current managed care climate, even those therapists with expertise in intimate partner abuse are often stymied by the insurance industry's short-term diagnostic requirements and reimbursement policies. Third, the growing dominance of evidence-based therapies has narrowed the definition of therapeutic success in ways that are counterproductive for many battered women. Finally, despite the promise of feminist therapy, considerable tension remains between mental health providers and agency-based advocates, and collaborations are few and far between (Gomez & Yassen, 2007; Lundy & Grossman, 2001).

Insufficient Training

Many mental health practitioners who work outside domestic violence-specific programs are poorly trained to screen for or respond to intimate partner violence. Battered women who come to mental health settings who complain of depression, substance abuse, anxiety, or marital difficulties often do not mention that they are being abused. Therapists, in turn, often fail to ask questions that would bring intimate partner violence to the foreground (Agar & Read, 2002; Harway & Hansen, 1993). In response, a victim may sense that the violence is off-limits for discussion or too shameful to mention, leaving therapists with a confusing picture from which important pieces are missing.

When battered women do seek therapy to address partner violence, therapists often are poorly equipped to respond effectively. Little research is available to guide the development of mental health interventions for survivors, and few mental health training programs mandate domestic violence training for their students (Chalk & King, 1998). One recent survey of psychiatry and doctoral-level psychology programs found that the vast majority of respondent schools did not require any training in interpersonal violence, although almost all participants believed they should do so (V. Kelly, 1997).

Rigid Reimbursement Criteria

Even when mental health providers are equipped to respond to domestic violence victims, they face a wide range of obstacles rooted in the dominant managed care system. For example, most insurance companies refuse reimbursement for psychotherapy sessions if a client has no psychiatric diagnosis (Warshaw & Moroney, 2002). As feminist therapist and scholar L. S. Brown (2005) has written, "[We] live in an era where . . . the norm is to find the most pathological *DSM* diagnosis possible so that services for a particular client will be funded" (p. 3). But many mental health providers perceive their survivor clients as coping in the best way they can with devastating external events. As noted previously, these therapists object to diagnostic labels that place responsibility on the client, rather than on the external obstacles she faces.

One counselor described her struggle with the diagnosis requirement this way:

> The extent to which a diagnosis is useful depends on the woman's
> culture, education, and access to information. If a domestic violence
> survivor is White and middle class and has the education and cultural

resources to think about the medical model in a critical way, she may feel that a diagnosis is normalizing and empowering because she is able to dismiss the "illness" connotation and focus on the fact that she is not alone in feeling the way she feels. But for someone who has never had the opportunity to think critically about the medical model, or who comes from a culture where people needing help for mental illness are marginalized, a diagnosis may make her feel judged, stigmatized, and damaged. (Susan Marine, personal communication, December 12, 2006)

Many therapists, particularly those practicing from a feminist perspective, agree that the diagnosis requirement sometimes puts them in a difficult bind. On the one hand, they are reluctant to impose a pathologizing label on a struggling client; on the other, the diagnostic label may be the client's only ticket to the assistance she needs.

Additionally, in a relatively short period of time, managed care companies have redefined mental health care as brief treatment for discrete disorders (L. S. Brown, 2005; McWilliams, 2005). Because therapy with trauma survivors builds on a gradually developed, trusting victim–therapist relationship, it is not easily adapted to fit such short time frames (Bonisteel & Green, 2005; Warshaw & Moroney, 2002). Effective mental health interventions are likely to extend beyond the number of sessions reimbursable by most managed care companies and many state assistance programs, placing them off limits to the women who need them most— those whose financial situations are precarious and who are therefore dependent on a battering partner.

Narrow Definitions of Success

Finally, throughout the mental health system, insurers are increasing their demands for *evidence-based* therapies—those that are based on quantitative empirical research that demonstrate success in achieving relatively short-term researcher-defined outcomes with highly specific client populations. Evidence-based interventions are highly structured, short term, and narrowly targeted to address a well-defined set of symptoms (McWilliams, 2005; Norcross, 2005).

Although it is appropriate in certain situations to prefer empirically derived, highly specific techniques, the growing dominance of such interventions substantially limits practitioners' freedom to respond to a client's individual needs (Bonisteel & Green, 2005; L. S. Brown, 2005; McWilliams, 2005). Many mental health providers prefer to allow clients to develop their own goals, to collaborate in the therapy process, and to work at their own pace. These practitioners operate from a knowledge base grounded in research that shows that the therapist–client relationship has a greater impact on a client's well-being than any other aspect of treatment (L. S. Brown, 2005). Such knowledge is increasingly devalued in the current climate.

Absence of Collaboration

Although feminist therapy practitioners have worked hard to develop collaborative relationships with advocates in domestic violence agencies, most mental health services providers practice in isolation, and considerable tension continues to exist between the two groups. As Susan Schechter (2000) has noted,

> Domestic violence agency staff and allied professionals often have little understanding of each other's roles, organizational and statutory mandates, professional limitations and ethical obligations. . . . Many communities have few—if any—mechanisms to support professionals to work collaboratively. . . . While there is lip service paid to the importance of collaboration, there seems to be little time and few training opportunities to make these complicated processes work. (p. 3)

CONCLUSION

Psychological theorizing about battered women has come a long way since the 1960s, when victim-blaming theories abounded. However, tension remains between those who emphasize the internal psychological needs of survivors and those whose primary concerns center on victims' practical needs and the sociopolitical causes of domestic violence. Although this divide between external political empowerment and internal psychological perspectives has begun to narrow in recent years, especially with the infusion of feminist therapy principles into the work of mainstream practitioners, more remains to be done. Mental health services providers need to advocate for domestic violence training in professional schools; for the elimination of pathologizing diagnoses as a precondition for services; for the reimbursement of longer term and more flexible therapeutic approaches; and for evaluation methodologies that allow for more varied and woman-centered definitions of success. Much work also remains to be done to promote collaboration between lay advocates and mental health professionals who work with domestic violence survivors. Battered women will be better served when lay advocates and mental health professionals operate from the premise that psychological experiences can be best understood within a sociopolitical and structural perspective and that an analysis of political disempowerment is deepened through exploration of its psychological impact on individuals (Goodman et al., 2005), that neither advocacy nor therapy alone can effectively address the issues most battered women face, that the political and the personal aspects of battering are deeply intertwined, and that effective eradication of domestic violence requires that attention be paid to both (Warshaw & Moroney, 2002).

4

The Justice
System Response

Into the 1970s, justice system officials such as police officers, prosecutors, and judges failed to recognize that there was a criminal dimension to partner violence. As the battered woman's movement grew, reforming this unresponsive but crucial system became one of its top priorities. Advocates in the early 1970s began demanding that the legal system treat domestic violence "like any other crime" rather than as a relationship problem. Since then, activists have transformed the justice system's response in three fundamental ways. First, they secured the adoption of criminal mandatory arrest laws and no-drop prosecution policies. Second, they persuaded state legislatures to enact laws that authorize civil protection orders for battered women. Third, they expanded the scope of the criminal justice system's response to survivors through new collaborations between government officials and private community partners. Despite this enormously successful transformation of the justice system, each of these reforms, in turn, created new and unanticipated challenges for battered women. Chapter 4 analyzes these changes and their consequences.

THE CRIMINAL JUSTICE SYSTEM

Until the 1990s, police officers typically failed to recognize intimate partner abuse as a criminal act, ignoring domestic violence calls or delaying any response by several hours. When a woman called 911 to report that "my boyfriend is mad at me and is going to beat me up," she would often be told, "Call us again when he does" (Cumming, 1965). When officers did respond, they were trained to mediate and to "avoid arrest if possible" (Eisenberg & Micklow, 1974). Arrests were rare; studies estimate that they occurred in only 3% to 14% of all intimate partner violence cases to which officers actually responded (Buzawa & Buzawa, 1992). Battered women were left with little or no access to the criminal justice system.

All of this changed following the publication of a highly touted and well-publicized research effort, the Minneapolis Domestic Violence Experiment (Sherman & Berk, 1984). The study, which concluded that arrest dramatically reduced the risk of reassault against the same victim during a 6-month period, had a profound influence on public policy (Sherman & Berk, 1984).[1] In 1984, the same year the study's results were published, the U.S. Attorney General's Task Force on Family Violence issued a report (U.S. Department of Justice, 1984) that recommended using arrest as the standard response to all cases of misdemeanor domestic assault.

In response to these pressures, states began to enact laws that required arrest in domestic abuse cases. Oregon passed the first mandatory arrest statute in 1977, and other states soon followed suit. By 2005, 26 states and the District of Columbia either required arrest or had adopted a proarrest policy (Miccio, 2005).

Mandatory arrest policies dramatically increased arrest rates for intimate partner violence. Consider the experience of one community, the District of Columbia. A study conducted in 1990 showed that police were arresting accused batterers in only 5% of cases where domestic violence victims called 911. They failed to arrest in more than 85% of cases where the victim had sustained serious injuries that were visible to the officer arriving on the scene (Sands, Baker, & Cahn, 1990). Four years after the local mandatory arrest law went into effect, arrest rates had increased from 5% to 41% (Keilitz, 1997). This change had a profound impact on sur-

---

[1] Since the original Minneapolis study, a number of additional studies have analyzed the impact of arrest. A reanalysis of the pooled data from these studies showed that unemployed perpetrators are more likely to be arrested for reassaulting a victim than are those who are employed. Researchers have theorized that the difference could stem from a lower "stake in conformity" on the part of unemployed batterers or from a lower likelihood that survivors will call the police in cases where the batterer or his family has more to lose (Maxwell, Garner, & Fagan, 1999; Wooldredge & Thistlethwaite, 2002).

vivors: Those who sought access to the criminal justice system were far more likely to succeed with the advent of mandatory arrest.

The police were not the only sector of the criminal justice community that had failed to take domestic violence seriously. Prosecutors often actively discouraged victims from pursuing cases against perpetrators. Even when mandatory arrest laws increased the number of domestic violence incidents brought to their attention, prosecutors rarely pressed charges and, when they did, they rarely followed through and took the case to trial (e.g., Epstein, 1999). In addition, domestic violence crimes were notoriously undercharged; a National Crime Survey (National Institute of Justice, 1990) found that over one third of misdemeanor partner abuse cases would have been charged as far more serious felony rapes, robberies, or aggravated assaults if they had been committed by strangers. The experience of Washington, DC, is again informative. In 1995, 15% of those arrested for partner violence were charged with a crime compared with 67% of those arrested for violence against strangers (Skolnik, 1997).

Why such a low number? Although it is generally the case that criminal charges can be filed or dropped only by prosecutors, not by victims, Washington, DC—along with most jurisdictions across the country—had adopted a special intimate abuse policy: Charges would be dropped at the victim's request, at any time, no questions asked (Epstein, 1999). District attorneys nationwide explained that "because victims simply do not follow through in domestic violence cases, there is no need to waste precious prosecutorial resources on them" (Cahn, 1992, p. 163).

This "automatic drop" policy ceded to perpetrators an enormous degree of control over the criminal justice process. All a batterer had to do was coerce his victim—through threats, violence, guilt, or apologies—into asking the prosecutor to drop the charges; once she did so, there was no longer a risk of jail time or a disincentive to batter. Although some prosecutors recognized that batterers might be pressuring victims into making the request to drop charges, they reported being unable to distinguish between a battered woman who was communicating her true feelings and one who had a literal or figurative gun to her head. Therefore, the government adopted a uniform approach and dropped charges in every case where a woman requested it (Epstein, 1999; see Rebovich, 1996, pp. 182–183).

During the 1980s and 1990s, advocates began to make inroads in changing these policies. In a growing number of states, prosecutors adopted no-drop policies. Once charges are brought, a case proceeds regardless of the victim's wishes as long as sufficient evidence exists to prove criminal conduct. Such evidence can include recorded calls to 911, photographs and hospital records that document injuries, and testimony from eyewitnesses or police officers who responded to the crime scene. Even in cases where the victim refuses to cooperate with the government or recants her original story and testifies for the defense, prosecuting attorneys often persevere, relying on these alternative sources of evidence.

As with mandatory arrest, no-drop prosecution strategies proved quite successful in improving victims' access to justice. Looking again at Washington, DC, the no-drop policy resulted in a radical shift in the rate of domestic violence prosecutions. In 1989, the United States Attorney's Office pursued fewer than 40 intimate partner violence misdemeanor cases. During the first year of the new regime, from mid-1995 to mid-1996, that number jumped to approximately 4,500 cases (Epstein, 1999). Since then, the office routinely has pressed charges in approximately 67% of arrest cases—precisely the same rate as in stranger violence cases (Kelly Higashi, personal communication, May 21, 2004; see also Skolnik, 1997).

Mandatory arrest laws and no-drop prosecution policies have moved domestic violence criminal prosecutions to a position of rough parity with crimes perpetrated by strangers and have greatly expanded the range of tools available to battered women who seek to escape abuse. These policies also represent an important symbolic shift: a clear declaration by the state that it no longer condones domestic violence (Ferraro & Pope, 1993; Ford & Regoli, 1993). Also, some scholars and activists argue that no-drop prosecution is the most effective way to prevent a perpetrator from escaping punishment by threatening victims into dropping charges (Hanna, 1996). This progress toward treating domestic violence like any other crime, however, has come at a substantial price.

INFLEXIBILITY OF CRIMINAL JUSTICE REFORMS
AND THE SILENCING OF WOMEN'S VOICES

Given the enormous complexity of intimate partner violence, no single response can meet the needs of every woman, and many responses that are well-suited to one situation can worsen another. Mandatory arrest laws and no-drop prosecution policies are designed on a one-size-fits-all model that lacks sufficient flexibility to respond effectively to particularized situations and leaves no room for contextualized understanding of an individual battered woman's life circumstances.[2] Once a woman, or a neighbor or friend, makes an initial call to the police, the victim is swept into a process over which she has little control. Her own wishes and needs become largely irrelevant to that process, even when she fears that prosecution will provoke the batterer into retaliatory abuse against her, when she needs her partner's economic support to keep her family afloat, or when she fears that her partner will be deported as a result of the prosecution.

The fundamental unresponsiveness of mandatory policies to women's individual needs and wishes is disempowering and dangerous for some victims. For example, 20% to 30% of arrested offenders reassault their partners before the court process has concluded or shortly afterward, often as retaliation for involving them in the court system (M. A. Finn, 2003; Ford & Regoli, 1992; Goodman, Bennett, & Dutton, 1999; Hart, 1996). Also, a National Institute of Justice study found that increased prosecution rates for domestic assault were associated with increased levels of homicides among White married couples, Black unmarried couples, and White unmarried women, even when controlling for other relevant variables (Dugan, Nagin, & Rosenfeld, 2001). Another risk stems from the fact that the sentencing of convicted domestic violence offenders tends to be relatively lenient, and few offenders are sentenced to serve any time in jail (Hemmens, Strom, & Schlegel, 1998; Miethe, 1987; Sherman, 1993). Even when an offender does receive a prison sentence, his sentence term is likely to be shorter than it would be for other types of offenders (Erez & Tontodonato, 1990).

---

[2] The tension between the general and the particular in feminist lawmaking on behalf of battered women was first explored by Elizabeth Schneider (see, e.g., Schneider, 2000).

Substantial data show that separation from the batterer is the time of greatest risk of serious violence and homicide for battered women and for their children (Fleury, Sullivan, & Bybee, 2000). Victims who choose to remain in an abusive relationship actually may be protecting their children as best they can, despite official notions of how a "good" mother would act in such circumstances. Still, prosecutors regularly subpoena victims and force them to testify (Epstein, 2002; Epstein, Bell, & Goodman, 2003; Mills, 1999). In some states, prosecutors have even threatened victims that if they failed to cooperate with the prosecution they would be jailed or their case would be referred to child protective services and they might lose their children (Epstein, 1999; Maxian, 2000). As one example, in Albany, New York, a victim refused to testify for the prosecution because of her extreme fear of her former boyfriend and her previous experiences with the criminal justice system's failure to offer her meaningful assistance. At the prosecutor's request, the judge held the woman in contempt of court and imprisoned her for an entire week (A. Klein, 2004, pp. 4–6).

Beyond the fear of retaliation, women may have many other reasons for wanting to drop criminal charges against their abusive partners. Chief among the reasons is a lack of sufficient economic resources to survive without them. Victims may well seek to drop charges so that the fathers of their children can continue to work and provide them with financial support. However, prosecutors are likely to reason that dropping the case would not serve the interests of the state in deterring future batterers from harming women. After all, it sends a mixed message, at best, if charges can be dropped for batterers whose families need their income. Prosecutors typically refuse to drop charges in such situations, and they are also unlikely to offer women any meaningful assistance in improving their financial situation; such services are few and far between.

Another problem with no-drop prosecution policies is that by coercing victims' participation in the prosecution, the government may teach them to distrust the criminal justice system in general. This experience may well make them far less likely to contact police or prosecutors in the future, which in turn may leave them more trapped than ever in their violent homes. Empirical evidence suggests that victims frequently avoid community interventions that fail to acknowledge the realities and intricacies of their lives (Baker, 1997). Similarly, extensive data demonstrate a strong link between people's perceptions of fair treatment in the justice system and their sense of the overall legitimacy of governmental authority. The more they feel heard, understood, and treated with fairness and respect, the more likely it is that they will seek police and prosecutorial assistance in the future (Epstein, 2002). The criminal justice system's lack of flexibility and individual responsiveness thwarts survivors' efforts to regain control over their lives, to move past abusive experiences, and to protect themselves from future violence.

The inflexibility of these government policies can be especially problematic for certain categories of victims, such as immigrant women, who realistically fear that their partners will be deported as a result of the prosecution, and women of color, who want to protect themselves and their communities from potential racism in the justice system. As one example, federal law provides that immigrants convicted of a domestic violence offense become deportable, even if they have previously obtained lawful permanent resident status (Omnibus Consolidated Appropriations Act, 2006).[3] Many women partnered with such men are reluctant to risk triggering deportation and being ostracized from their communities for doing so, particularly if the perpetrators might be subjected to political persecution if forced to return to their home countries. Faced with rigid policy mandates, these women often choose to remain silent about abuse (Loke, 1997).

Similarly, African American women often are reluctant to involve the police in domestic disputes, particularly when this entails participating in a criminal justice system that has historically failed to provide equal justice to people of color. Kimberlé Crenshaw (1991), whose writing has explored the "intersectionality" of experiences of racism and sexism, noted a general

> unwillingness among people of color to subject their private lives to
> the scrutiny and control of a police force that is frequently hostile.

---

[3] This law also allows for deportation of any immigrant who violates the portion of a protection order that involves protection against credible threats of violence, repeated harassment, or bodily injury (Omnibus Consolidated Appropriations Act, 2006).

There is also a more generalized community ethic against public intervention, the product of a desire to create a private world free from the diverse assaults on the public lives of racially subordinated people. The home is not simply a man's castle in the patriarchal sense, but may also function as a safe haven from the indignities of life in a racist society. (p. 1257)

This reluctance has only increased in recent years, as women of color "experience the negative effects of conservative legislation regarding public assistance, affirmative action, and immigration" (Richie, 2000, p. 1135). Victims whose experience has led them to expect to encounter racism in the criminal justice system are far less likely to turn to the police for assistance (Websdale, 2001).

Given the number of women for whom mandatory policies appear problematic, it is not surprising that research has failed to show clear positive results. Studies now show that mandatory arrest has, at best, a mixed impact on reducing intimate partner violence (Bennett Cattaneo & Goodman, 2005; Maxwell, Garner, & Fagan, 1999). Although no rigorous outcome study of no-drop prosecution has been conducted, researchers have found that victims who followed through with prosecution were less likely to experience subsequent violence only if they made a personal choice to participate and were not coerced into doing so (Ford & Regoli, 1992). Other research has shown that women who experience government officials as listening to their stories and responding to their individual needs are more likely to feel treated fairly and therefore to cooperate with prosecutors' requests than are women who feel forced into a mandatory model dismissive of their input (Erez & Belknap, 1998; Ford & Regoli, 1993). As a result, despite most advocates' initial enthusiasm, concern is steadily growing about the degree to which these policies actually keep women safe (see, e.g., Davies, Lyon, & Monti-Catania, 1998; Epstein, 2002; Mills, 1998).

THE CIVIL JUSTICE SYSTEM

Frustrated with the slow pace of reform among police and prosecutors, in the late 1960s and early 1970s activists turned their attention to creating protections for battered women in the civil justice system. They persuaded legislatures to adopt protection order statutes, which are specially tailored to meet the essential safety needs of battered women. These laws authorize judges to create flexible individually responsive solutions and to increase survivors' access to justice by allowing them to file cases directly, on their own behalf. Today, every state has a protection order statute, though eligibility criteria and the scope of available protections differ (DeJong & Burgess-Proctor, 2006; Epstein, 1999). Protection orders (also called *restraining orders, domestic violence orders,* and *peace bonds*) can direct a batterer to avoid any kind of contact with a victim and to refrain from assaulting or threatening her. In addition, these orders may contain directives concerning custody, visitation arrangements, child support, and access to housing (Epstein, 1999; Logan, Shannon, & Walker, 2005).

Rapid resolution of these latter issues is critical. One of the primary reasons victims return to their abusive partners is the pressure created by the loss of economic support (e.g., Bybee & Sullivan, 2002); for a woman with children, a child support award may be the key to freedom. Similarly, because the potential for renewed violence is particularly acute during visitation, carefully structured pick-up and drop-off provisions designed to eliminate victim–perpetrator contact also can significantly reduce the risk of future violence (P. Finn & Colson, 1990).

In contrast to criminal prosecution, protection order laws were developed expressly to provide more flexible individually tailored legal remedies for battered women. The District of Columbia's civil protection order statute, for example, authorizes judges to award any relief that is "appropriate to the effective resolution of the matter" (District of Columbia Court Reorganization Act of 1970). A perpetrator might be ordered to attend parenting counseling, provide spousal support, reimburse the victim for injury-related medical bills, relinquish the children's passports, refrain from contacting the victim's employer, or be subject to other situation-specific remedies. In most states, these orders remain in effect for 1 to 3 years and may be extended on demonstration of continued need. In addition, every state has adopted criminal enforcement mechanisms for protection orders (Epstein, 2002). Although the data are mixed, several of the most rigorous studies indicate that those women who obtained a permanent order reported considerably less reabuse over time compared with those who reported an incident to the police but did not file for a protection order (Holt, Kernic, Lumley, Wolf, & Rivara, 2002; Holt, Kernic, Wolf, & Rivara, 2003; for a recent review of the literature, see Logan, Shannon, Walker, & Faragher, 2006).

PUNISHING NONCONFORMITY IN THE CIVIL PROTECTION ORDER PROCESS

Although the civil protection order system is far more responsive and individually tailored to the needs of battered women than its criminal justice counterpart, it has its share of problems as well. Perhaps the primary one is that protection orders often are not enforced, particularly in cases where police perceive victim risk to be relatively low (P. Finn, 1989; Kane, 2000). Frequently, police still refuse to arrest a batterer who has violated a protection order, even when the victim begs them to do so. This practice can substantially undermine a woman's faith in the justice system, making her much less likely to rely on it in the future. Why should she risk her abusive partner's wrath when the protective order turns out to be "nothing but a piece of paper," just as he told her it was?

Another significant problem is that in practice, the civil protection order system rests on the assumption that all survivors wish—or should wish—to exit their abusive relationships. However, as previously discussed, women may have numerous reasons for choosing to stay in such a relationship, including economic necessity, fear, and cultural pressure. Women who rely on their abusive partners for financial support, child care, or housing may not be able to survive without continued contact. As a result, they may want the violence to stop but not yet be ready to end the relationship. These women need support in their efforts to become more economically self-reliant, but such assistance is not offered by the justice system or by most community programs (Logan et al., 2006). Immigrant women may be particularly unlikely to choose separation from their partners for reasons having to do with religion, tradition, economic dependence, or a desire to remain part of a community that would not condone such an action.

By assuming that all battered women need to end their relationships, judges in civil cases often are substituting their own judgment for that of the victims who are seeking assistance in their courtrooms. As one example, in Washington, DC, a victim obtained a protection order that directed her abusive boyfriend not to harm or threaten her, not to contact her, and to stay away from her. Several months later, while the order was still in effect, she returned to court to tell the judge that the situation had changed, that she no longer needed the court's assistance, and that she wanted the order to be vacated. The judge asked her whether her boyfriend, who was not present at the hearing, had coerced her into making the request; she testified that he had not. The judge concluded that the woman had failed to provide sufficient reason to vacate the protection order and denied her request. As she explained from the bench, "You can't just open the door to the state, getting the state involved, and then think that you can shut it at any time" (Tammy Kuennen [petitioner's attorney], personal communication, April 2006).

Other judges have fined or imprisoned battered women for initiating contact with an abusive partner during the effective period of a protection order (e.g., Clines, 2002; Goodmark, 2003; Simon, 2002). In Newark, Ohio, for example, Betty Lucas obtained a protection order against her abusive husband, which included a provision that directed him to stay away from her and her home. When she later held a birthday party for one of their children, she allowed her husband to attend. The couple began fighting and the police came to the scene. Lucas was criminally charged with "aiding and abetting" her abusive partner's violation of her protection order. In the judge's view, she had *"recklessly exposed herself* [italics added] to the offender from whom she had sought protection" (*State v. Lucas*, 2002). Lucas was sentenced to 90 days in jail; her husband, who had actually committed the violation, got off with a $100 fine. Although the Ohio Supreme Court ultimately overturned Lucas's conviction, this case and others like it demonstrate how little tolerance judges in civil protection order cases have for women who do not conform to state expectations as well as how willing judges are to use criminal sanctions to enforce officially "appropriate" behavior.

This pressure toward separation is particularly problematic when juxtaposed with evidence that many judges who preside over contested custody proceedings fail to credit or refuse to consider allegations of intimate partner violence. Instead, these judges emphasize the importance of dual parent involvement and award joint custody—thus forcing survivors to maintain unwanted close contact with abusive partners (Goodmark, 1999; Meier, 2003).[4] Survivors thus find themselves at the receiving end of deeply inconsistent judicial messages—you must separate from your abusive partner, regardless of your preference; except if you have children, in which case you must remain in regular contact with him even if you wish to leave. Both approaches wrest control away from the victim.

As these stories illustrate, civil judges, like their criminal justice counterparts, often use their considerable power to control the lives of victims. Even assuming that such judicial actions stem from the best intentions—an effort to do everything possible to keep battered women safe—this regular undermining of battered women's autonomy is deeply problematic.

COORDINATED COMMUNITY RESPONSES

As increasing resources and attention began to be devoted to the criminal justice system's response to battered women, advocates started to search for ways to become involved in its routine operations. The most successful of these efforts has been the creation of *coordinated community responses*. As discussed below, coordination has come in the form of interagency communication, colocation of services for battered women, and unified domestic violence courts.

Interagency Communication

In 1980, advocates in Duluth, Minnesota, initiated the Domestic Abuse Intervention Project, the first formal, coordinated community response to domestic violence (Pence & Shepard, 1999). They brought police, pros-

---

[4] Joint custody awards are frequently made even in states where legislation prohibits such a ruling if adult-on-adult violence is proven (Meier, 2003).

ecutors, judges, and other court personnel together with anti–domestic violence advocates and social service providers to cross-train and coordinate their responses to cases of intimate partner abuse. As part of this process, advocates convinced officials throughout the criminal justice system to rethink their policies to enhance the safety of battered women. Advocates then led an intensive effort to foster interdisciplinary collaboration and design interagency procedures to further this goal. In the words of Ellen Pence (2001), one of the program's founders,

> We found opportunities to enhance women's safety in dispatch and patrol response procedures, booking procedures and bail hearings; when decisions were being made to prosecute, defer, or drop a case; during pretrial maneuvers, trial tactics, sentencing hearings, and revocations of probation. . . . We proposed new legislation, new notions of practitioners' job duties, new department policies, new interagency protocols, and new administrative forms. (p. 338)

The coordinated community response model substantially reshaped the Duluth criminal justice system's approach to domestic violence crimes.

On the basis of the success of this early effort, in 1987 the National Center for Juvenile and Family Court Judges held a national conference, bringing together interdisciplinary teams from every state to discuss the potential impact of coordinated community responses. Team members returned to their home states excited and energized about the benefits of coordination. However, the model promoted at this influential conference and rapidly replicated across the country represented a significant shift away from Duluth's advocate-led program (Pence, 2001). Team members pushed for the formation of Family Violence Coordinating Councils as the policymaking centers for coordinated community responses. Although all government and private providers could participate as members, these councils typically were hosted and chaired not by advocates but by judges, prosecutors, governors, or mayors (Edwards, 1992; National Council of Juvenile and Family Court Judges, 1990). Advocates constituted only one voice at the table, a far cry from their Duluth role as the principal architects of reform. The move toward state leadership resulted in councils focused on "efficiency, arrests, and convictions [rather] than on critiquing the impact of institutional responses on the safety, autonomy, and integrity of battered women" (Pence, 2001, p. 337).

Despite this limitation, coordinated community responses succeeded in bringing together agencies that previously had rarely, if ever, communicated about their work. Family violence councils provided opportunities for lawyers to talk to health care providers about how important properly documented medical records can be to a successful trial; for probation officers to talk to counselors about how to obtain victims' perspectives on their abusive partners' responsiveness to treatment; and for judges to hear from advocates about how better to understand the behavior of battered women in their courtrooms (Shepard & Pence, 1999). Coordinated community responses continue to be the centerpiece of reform efforts for the domestic violence criminal justice system nationwide.

Colocated Services

In addition to coordinating procedures, many family violence councils have promoted comprehensive provision of services to battered women at a single site. These sites are designed to provide a wide range of criminal justice system, medical, counseling, and social services to battered women in a single convenient location. Colocation of services can help to improve battered women's access to assistance, limit the number of times a victim must repeat her story to different service providers, and foster interdisciplinary collaboration with an eye toward increased safety (see Epstein, 1999). In 2004, the U.S. Department of Justice awarded $20 million to help 12 communities develop such centers (U.S. Department of Justice, 2004); they are proliferating in communities dedicated to domestic violence reform.

Unified Domestic Violence Courts

A third major coordination effort that grew out of family violence councils was the creation of unified domestic violence courts. Although such courts are structured in a variety of ways, they typically include (a) a limited number of judicial officers who hear only domestic violence cases and receive specialized training, (b) partnerships between the court and community agencies to improve service provision, (c) in-court advocacy services, (d) efforts to make the court system more accessible and less onerous for victims, and (e) efforts to increase the consistency of court orders that affect a single family (Epstein, 1999). Some unified domestic violence courts have brought together civil and criminal cases into a single unit, coordinating calendars so that victims need to appear less frequently and can better understand the judicial process (Epstein, 1999). Others have brought together protection order and family law cases, such as divorce and custody, helping to improve access to both short- and long-term relief for families (Epstein, 1999).

To some extent, these developments appear to be working. One large-scale study of women in the justice system found that the more battered women perceived different agencies as working together, the more highly they rated them in terms of helpfulness and effectiveness and the more satisfied they were both with the legal system in general and with their own individual case outcomes in particular (Zweig & Burt, 2006).

THE SUBORDINATION OF BATTERED WOMEN AND THEIR ADVOCATES IN COORDINATED RESPONSES

Despite these improvements, at least two major limitations thwart the potential of coordinated responses: the relative subordination of battered women's advocates and the absence of attention to women's individual stories and needs. The history of the Abused Women's Active Response Emergency (AWARE) program, implemented in the Netherlands, Canada, and several U.S. communities, illustrates the first of these issues. AWARE was designed to facilitate the arrest of perpetrators and to protect and support stalking victims. Women participants have their homes wired with an electronic alarm system that can be activated by pushing a button in the house or on a pendant that they carry with them. The program is run by a coordinated interdisciplinary team of police, prosecutors, social workers, youth care workers, and battered women's shelter representatives. Police officers agree to prioritize these alarm calls, and other program participants agree to provide counseling and social work services in conjunction with criminal justice intervention.

Despite the program's conceptualization as an interdisciplinary collaboration, an in-depth evaluation revealed that the interests and values of justice system actors rapidly trumped those of other program participants (Romkens, 2006). The social work and youth care officials, who are more likely to directly represent the victims' needs as opposed to those of the state,

> often deferred to the legal professionals on the committee (police and/or lawyers). They usually emphasized their role on the committee as secondary and as helping the legal actors. . . . Arguments of social workers were regularly qualified as more "personal," less convincing, and not as "strong" as what counted as legal documents and/or arguments. For example, in the absence of police records on prior incidents, medical records or social work information on prior abuse that women had suffered were considered not objective enough. . . . In effect, with this deferential attitude, the nonlegal participants in the program actively colluded in setting up a hierarchy in the process of decision making that went beyond any difference in responsibility among the various participants. (Romkens, 2006, p. 173)

These findings demonstrate that coordinated community responses must go beyond simply bringing organizations together. Instead, they must make efforts to equalize power and promote mutual respect across disciplines so that victims' needs can be given appropriate weight (Romkens, 2006).

Just as advocates are not given equal power and respect in many coordinated responses, so too are victims themselves relegated to a peripheral status. Although their criminal cases are aggressively pursued, centralized access to a variety of resources is available, and case logistics are more likely to be coordinated, there are still few opportunities for victims to communicate their own goals, desires, material needs, and safety concerns to system actors with the power to dramatically affect their lives. This is because most, if not all, community response efforts are limited to coordinating the procedural aspects of the cases and the resources available to victims. They are not designed to facilitate a coordinated effort among system actors that is individually tailored to the needs of any particular battered woman. This structure parallels the dominant approach prevalent in the advocacy community (see chap. 2, this volume); it is service, rather than survivor, defined. Improved policies, streamlined processes, and coordinated court dates are an important first step in protecting battered women. However, to be truly effective, interdisciplinary initiatives need to increase police, prosecutorial, and judicial openness to individual victim involvement in shaping the goals to be pursued in their individual cases.

CONCLUSION

Despite the advantages brought by mandatory arrest and prosecution policies, civil protection order statutes, and coordinated community responses, none of these policies are sufficiently geared toward responding to a woman's individual needs. Until the justice system is able to respond directly to the particular obstacles, needs, and goals of diverse battered women, the justice system will remain inaccessible or even harmful to many survivors of intimate partner violence.

5

A Critical Analysis of System Responses: The Importance of Voice, Community, and Economic Empowerment

Although our society has made substantial strides toward acknowledging the existence and importance of intimate partner violence and in improving its responsiveness to survivors (see chaps. 2–4, this volume), numerous obstacles to victim safety still exist. Much contemporary discussion about how to best meet the continuing challenges that survivors face is handicapped by the fact that most scholars and activists limit their analysis to a particular field, such as health care or criminal justice. In fact, critiques that have been developed within specific disciplines can be integrated to paint a richer and more comprehensive picture of existing obstacles. In chapter 5, we apply our essential critique—that it is time to move beyond the one-size-fits-all rigid responses that marginalize women's particular situations and perspectives—across the fields of advocacy, mental health, and civil and criminal justice. This discussion provides a conceptual framework for chapter 6 (this volume), where we recommend new strategies for the continuing fight against domestic violence.

OVERVIEW

Feminist theorists have long emphasized that women's lived experiences are not monolithic and universal but varied and highly context specific. The uniform nature of many contemporary responses to intimate partner violence offers little room for any such nuance. Existing interventions often rest on the assumption that all survivors have the same essential needs—those common to White, middle-class, heterosexual women. This view, described by feminist theorists as *gender essentialism*, applies the norms of the most privileged women to the entire gender (Bartky, 1997; Chamallas, 2003).

Future efforts must thoroughly integrate antiessentialist insights to build on successes in combating intimate partner violence. Those involved in the domestic violence movement can accomplish this goal by focusing on three major issues. First, we must honor the differences in survivors' particularized needs by creating opportunities for individuals to be heard and to play an active role in shaping the assistance they receive.

Second, we must recognize the importance of battered women's relationships and community ties. We need to ensure that every battered woman has the opportunity and ability to leave her relationship, receives sufficient counseling to make the most independent choice possible, and is fully informed about available alternatives. But we also need to understand and accept that some women will decide to continue a connection with an abusive partner and that they will need help in finding ways to increase their safety within this context. In addition, we must find ways to assist isolated women to create or reconnect with supportive social networks and to help other women expand and strengthen the positive community ties they already have.

Third, as we expand the range of resources available to battered women, we should focus on those whose socioeconomic status limits their opportunities to be safe. Economic empowerment is a crucial precondition to safety for many battered women.

INCLUSION OF
A SURVIVOR-DEFINED PERSPECTIVE

The concept of voice is central to feminist theory (Belenky, Clinchy, Goldberger, & Tarule, 1986; Bond, Belenky, & Weinstock, 2000; Gilligan, 1982). In the 1960s and 1970s, as women shared their experiences in consciousness-raising groups and other settings, they realized that gender subordination had severely curtailed their opportunities to publicly articulate and frame their own experiences as women (hooks, 1990). Many feminists viewed their central task as creating conditions in which women could speak for themselves (K. Brabeck, 2003) and discern and define their own needs (Gergen, 2001; S. Jackson, 1998). Over time, "voice" became "a kind of megametaphor representing presence, power, participation, protest, and identity" (Reinharz, 1994, p. 183).

In the early battered women's movement, listening to survivors was seen as a way of restoring their often damaged sense of self-esteem, personal power, and autonomy as well as an important source of information about how to most effectively combat abuse. Grassroots activists developed victim services based on the needs survivors expressed through consciousness-raising groups and crisis intervention counseling sessions. But the movement became increasingly dominated by professional service providers and expanded across a wide range of public and private service delivery systems that prized standardization. The diversity of survivors' particular circumstances became increasingly peripheral, and individual women lost a good deal of control over the decisions affecting their lives.

The standardization of domestic violence services over time diverted attention from the fact that victims—and their needs for services—differ on the basis of numerous factors, including mental and physical well-being; family structure; religious, ethnic, and cultural background; immigration status; sexual orientation; embeddedness in social networks; and socioeconomic status (Bartky, 1997; L. S. Brown, 1990; Russo & Vaz, 2001; Sokoloff & Dupont, 2005a). As psychologist Michelle Bograd (1999) has written, "A battered woman may judge herself and be judged by others differently if she is white or black, poor or wealthy, a prostitute or a housewife, a citizen or an undocumented immigrant" (p. 277). For some battered women, domestic violence may not even be the most pressing concern. No single response can meet the needs of every survivor, and failure to heed individual battered women's voices precludes many of them from receiving meaningful assistance.

The story of Maria, a recent immigrant from El Salvador, illustrates the problem.[1] When her husband, Robert, punched her in the eye, it was

---

[1] This is the story of a woman with whom one of the authors worked. The names and minor identifying details have been changed to protect individual privacy.

the first time he had used violence against her. Maria wanted to communicate clearly that although she was willing to give him another chance, she would not tolerate any future violence in the relationship. She called the police, hoping they would talk to Robert and send a strong deterrent message. She did not want Robert arrested, because an arrest record would cost him his job, and he was the primary source of financial support for Maria and her two children. Maria also was concerned that if her husband was convicted of a violent crime, he would be deported to their war-torn home country and she would be ostracized by her Salvadoran immigrant community for causing his deportation.

But Robert and Maria lived in a mandatory arrest jurisdiction. When the police arrived, they told her that they had no choice but to arrest him. If the same events had occurred between two buddies in a bar or between "brothers" in a fraternity house, the officers would have had the discretion to give them a stern talking-to and send them home, keeping the case out of the criminal justice system. In domestic violence cases, however, years of experience had taught system officials that they could not distinguish between a woman who means what she says (when she tells the police that all she needs is a little backup from the authorities but no arrest) and one who makes the same passionate plea solely because if she does not, she fears she will be subjected to more violence. Lacking the resources necessary to sort out these very different cases, reformers had opted for a simple but straightforward solution: always arrest.

But what about Maria, whose needs were ignored because the system's one-size-fits-all approach did not recognize them? She is likely to feel disserved or even betrayed by the police. Their actions may expose her to a wide range of future harms, including retaliatory violence, poverty, homelessness, and loss of community. As a result, Maria may well decline to call the police if she ever again finds herself subjected to intimate partner violence. Her friends, hearing her story, may well do the same. Because the criminal justice system failed to listen and respond to this woman's particular needs, she has lost a potentially useful tool in her effort to become safe.

No-drop prosecution policies operate in much the same way, facilitating access to the criminal justice system for those battered women who seek it but in the process also sweeping up many others who object to their forced involvement. Victim advocates employed by criminal justice agencies often have little ameliorative impact, because they typically must condition the provision of services on a woman's willingness to subordinate her own goals to the those of the police department or district attorney's office (see chap. 4, this volume).

Although the civil protection order system is far more responsive to the needs and desires of individual battered women, even there judges are increasingly comfortable substituting their own judgment for that of a battered woman pleading her case. In the mental health system, where posttraumatic stress disorder is the reigning diagnosis and short-term, symptom-focused approaches are the available mainstream interventions, battered women often have little control over the ways their experiences are understood or addressed (see chaps. 3 and 4, this volume).

Even shelters and the services they offer have become largely untethered from their woman-centered roots. This shift was driven, in large part, by funders. Private foundations and government agencies require shelters to demonstrate success in terms of narrow predetermined results, such as the percentage of program "clients" who leave their abusive partners, obtain a protection order, find alternative shelter, or engage with other community agencies for additional services (Bonisteel & Green, 2005; Schechter, 1982). Funder preferences also catalyzed a move toward increasingly professionalized staffing, leading to a specialized narrow service focus. Both of these changes led to a system that is far less responsive to battered women with multiple complex problems (see chap. 2, this volume).

Although all of these services—criminal prosecutions, protection orders, mainstream mental health interventions, and system-based advocacy—are intended to assist and empower battered women, their inflexibility and lack of survivor centeredness can profoundly disempower victims. Survivors who are forced into these inflexible models may well reject them altogether (Smyth, Goodman, & Glenn, 2006). For a woman who finds system-based resources so unresponsive that she chooses to avoid them, there are few places to turn for help, and in the absence of nuanced intervention, she may well face continuing or escalating violence (Anderson, 2003; Johnson & Hotton, 2003; Rennison & Welchans, 2000).

A small but growing body of research on survivors' experiences of control over their own choices illustrates another danger of this trend away from listening to women's voices. One study, for example, found that participants who reported feeling in control of the process of working with service providers were far more likely to rate the services they received as helpful and to use them again (Zweig, Burt, & Van Ness, 2003). Similarly, a study within the criminal justice system found that victims who chose not to report recidivist abuse to officials were those who felt they had "no voice" in a previous prosecution (Hotaling & Buzawa, 2003).

Future reform efforts must create genuine opportunities to amplify battered women's voices and their ability to control the decisions that affect their lives. The next generation of anti–domestic violence reform must be designed to assist a broader range of battered women and be sufficiently flexible to respond to their individual needs. In short, the battered women's movement must revisit its roots; it must refocus on supporting and empowering women and incorporating individual responsiveness into government and community programs.

Let us be clear: We do not advocate abandoning the gains that have been made on behalf of battered women seeking mainstream services. The criminal justice system, for example, cannot return to an era when prosecutors automatically dropped cases at the victim's request. Such policies cede far too much control to perpetrators of violence. However, it is now time to move beyond the other extreme, where women have virtually no influence over their cases. As Donna Coker (2001) explained, "The dilemma for feminists is to develop strategies for controlling state actors—ensuring that the police come when called and that prosecutors do not trivialize cases—without increasing state control *of women*" (p. 803). We as a society need to preserve the progress achieved for many, while attending to the unmet needs of those still left out by current practices. This can only be done by finding a more accommodating flexible middle ground.

Responding to battered women's individual needs is even more challenging than it first sounds because many victims, particularly those who have experienced the physical and psychological coercion of intimate terrorism, may be so completely in the thrall of their batterer that they have trouble exercising free choice or may appear to be acting irrationally.

Although women in these situations present the greatest challenge, even they retain some degree of agency, which can be nurtured and supported. Many victims face abuse that is not life threatening, such as those experiencing situational couple violence. These survivors are far more able to make independent choices, though they still may need varying levels of support to expand their sense of possibility and of the range of opportunities realistically available to them. Women in both groups will be safer if given the opportunity to maximize their own agency; as a result, providers need to make their best efforts to avoid a reflexive substitution of their own judgment for that of a survivor.

In light of these complexities, any viable solutions are certain to be resource intensive. But providing more individualized assistance with prevention and early intervention ultimately should prove less costly than the current policy of ignoring individual differences among survivors. If more battered women feel supported by existing systems, they—and their friends, relatives, and acquaintances—will be more likely to use available resources and to call on them again if violence recurs. Fewer survivors will choose to go underground, where nothing can be done to protect them and their children. Providing useful resources to a greater percentage of victims increases the probability of preventing recidivist violence (which itself entails enormous expense, as noted in chap. 1, this volume), which in turn would cut short the intergenerational cycle of abuse and move us substantially closer to eradicating domestic violence.

RELATIONSHIPS AND COMMUNITY EMBEDDEDNESS

Mainstream western psychology traditionally has prized separation, autonomy, and independence as objective indicators of psychological health and maturity. Feminist theorists and psychologists have criticized these standards as culture bound and limited (Gilligan, 1982; Jordan, 2001; Miller, 1987). They emphasize, instead, the centrality of relationships and community in human development and psychological functioning, positing that personal growth and positive change often occur through relationships with others, whether harmonious or conflictual

(Jordan & Hartling, 2002; Miller, 1987; Miller & Stiver, 1997; Sarason, Sarason, & Gurung, 2001). For example, the widely embraced relational–cultural theory rejects the development of a bounded autonomous self as the definition of psychological health (Miller, 1987; Miller & Stiver, 1997). Instead, it identifies mutual empathy and empowerment as markers of emotional well-being and chronic relational disconnection and isolation as the primary sources of human suffering (Jordan, 1997; West, 2005). Relational–cultural theorists observe that family, friends, and neighbors, as well as religious, cultural, and ethnic communities, are critical to individuals' sense of identity; their experience of being known, understood, and valued; and their sense of being part of something larger (Baker-Miller, 1993; Smyth et al., 2006). For all of these reasons, most people deeply value their intimate relationships and community connections.

However, as previously discussed, domestic violence service providers often require women to risk or even relinquish important relationships in order to receive services (Smyth et al., 2006). This process is more complex than it might sound: Women are not typically presented with these two options—services versus relationships—as a straightforward, binary choice. Most service providers struggle to provide a greater range of options within the confines of funder demands and available services. These advocates would gladly embrace a world in which battered women could pursue a broader range of paths, enabling them to help each individual achieve the best possible result under difficult circumstances. However, given existing resource limitations, advocates in most programs find it difficult to avoid offering their clients a fairly narrow set of choices.

The next section examines two common demands made of survivors. One is that they sever all ties with their abusive partner, and the other is that they remove themselves from the communities in which they live.

Relationships With Intimate Partners

When a battered woman seeks help from a police officer, a shelter worker, or another front-line responder, she typically is urged to end her relationship. Most service providers see a victim's immediate physical safety as their paramount goal and assume that this also is (or at least should be) the victim's top priority as well (J. Brown, 1997; Kim, 2002; O'Brien & Murdock, 1993). They further assume that terminating the relationship is the most efficient and certain way to ensure such safety. These assumptions stem, in part, from the idea—now challenged by research findings— that intimate partner violence always escalates in frequency and severity (Anderson, 2003; Baker, 1997; Campbell et al., 2003; Jacobson, Gottman, Gortner, Berns, & Shortt, 1996; H. Johnson, 2003; Peled, Eisikovitz, Enosh, & Winstok, 2000). This view is especially prevalent in the criminal justice system, where the batterer often is seen in a one-dimensional light—as a violent offender who must be held accountable—and women who decide to stay in their relationships are perceived as victims without agency (Baker, 1997; Kim, 2002; Peled et al., 2000).

Many women do, indeed, desperately wish to stop the abuse by ending their relationships, but they often must overcome a wide variety of practical obstacles to do so. These include the possibility of violent retaliation, dependence on an abusive partner for practical and financial resources, concern that he will take away her children, and anxiety that he will threaten or actually harm other relatives (Barnett, 2001; Browne, 1987; Butts Stahly, 1999; Erez & Belknap, 1998). Most service providers have a sophisticated understanding of these obstacles and work hard and effectively to help women overcome them.

Service providers tend to be less open to those survivors who want to stop the abuse but remain in their relationships (Peled et al., 2000). Some of these women emphasize their partner's good qualities and the positive aspects of their connection (Kearney, 2001). Others may be willing to risk future incidents of abuse for the sake of other things that they find more important, such as ensuring that their children continue to live with their fathers, keeping their children out of poverty, or adhering to specific cultural or religious traditions.

Together, these practical and relational considerations lead many abuse victims to remain with their abusive partners. Approximately one third of women who spend time in domestic violence shelters return to their partners immediately after leaving the shelter (Griffing et al., 2002; A. J. Martin et al., 2000); and within 2 months of leaving, over 60% have returned to their partners (Campbell et al., 1995; Campbell, Rose, Kub, &

Nedd, 1998; Strube & Barbour, 1984). In addition, a substantial proportion of women who leave their abusive partners return to them multiple times over the course of the relationship (M. E. Bell, Goodman, & Dutton, in press; Campbell & Soeken, 1999). Although this pattern of leaving and returning is often interpreted as evidence of progress toward permanent separation, it also demonstrates a woman's effort to create greater safety within the relationship by conveying to the abuser that separation is an option (Peled et al., 2000).

By deciding to stay with an abusive partner or by leaving and then returning, a woman may be pursuing the most logical strategic path to safety. Several studies have shown that abusive relationships can become safer over time (M. E. Bell et al., in press; Jacobson et al., 1996; H. Johnson, 2003). Studies of "separation violence" have found that abuse often is more frequent and more severe among women who have separated from their partners than among those still involved in their relationships (Anderson, 2003; Campbell et al., 2003; Hotton, 2001; H. Johnson & Hotton, 2003; Rennison & Welchans, 2000). These data show that increased safety may be possible within a continued relationship and that leaving is not always the answer.

The efforts of service providers and justice system officials to help women leave their partners when they wish to do so are critically important. But by placing such heavy emphasis on this option alone, providers fail to effectively serve those battered women who do not wish to leave, cannot realistically choose to do so, or are safer if they stay. As a result, these women may avoid interactions with the police or the courts, where jail time for the perpetrator in a criminal case or pressure to include a stay-away provision in a civil protection order runs directly counter to their interests. They also may choose to avoid shelters, many of which measure their residents' success by their continued separation from abusive partners after a shelter stay (Peled et al., 2000). Women who want the violence to end but the relationship to continue may be made to feel guilty or labeled as "noncompliant" (Smyth, Goodman, & Glenn, 2006). Service providers across disciplines tend to interpret a woman's decision to stay "as proof of disorganization and powerlessness, rather than a [possible] sign of her competence and coping" (Peled et al., 2000, p. 16).

Although it may seem counterintuitive, it is a simple truth that some battered women will return to, or never leave, their partners and that in some cases this may be the wisest choice. Unless society is prepared to abandon these women to a life of continued violence, advocacy efforts and system reform should evolve along two separate but related tracks. First, providers must continue to work to eradicate obstacles that prevent women who wish to leave from doing so. For some women, obstacles may be practical in nature; for others, the primary obstacle may be the challenge of moving beyond the thrall of an abusive partner's psychological control and reopening their minds to the possibility of a different, safer life. Women in the latter group are likely to need intensive counseling as well as sufficient time and safety to make a decision with which they can live in the long term. In addition, all battered women must receive counseling about the potential risks of remaining in an abusive relationship as well as information about resources that might help them to exit successfully and the risks that might stem from separation.

Second, programs that promote greater safety for women who choose to maintain connection with their partners must also be created (Yoshioka & Choi, 2005). Such programs will succeed only if they communicate nonjudgmental acceptance of a woman's choice, understanding of the complex circumstances in which that choice is made, and a way to remain connected to supportive resources in the future.

Embeddedness in Community

Although only some partner violence victims wish to maintain a relationship with their partners, connection to a larger, supportive community is vital to virtually all victims' physical safety (Goodman, Dutton, Vankos, & Weinfurt, 2005; Sullivan & Bybee, 1999) and psychological recovery (Carlson, McNutt, Choi, & Rose, 2002; Thompson, Kaslow, & Kingree, 2002). For some survivors, particularly immigrants, a community also may be necessary for basic survival. If a woman does not speak English and has few resources and limited marketable skills, a community of those who are similarly situated (or at least sympathetic to the challenges she faces) is essential.

Domestic violence victims typically turn to their own social networks and communities before accessing institutions such as domestic violence agencies, the mental health system, or the justice system (Lempert, 1996; Rose, Campbell, & Kub, 2000). In addition, because many women never seek assistance from institutional actors—three quarters of all physical assaults against women are not reported to the police (Tjaden & Thoennes, 2000)—community support plays a particularly crucial role. The reluctance to report is especially common in marginalized populations, whose members may distrust institutional actors. One study of predominantly African American battered women, for example, found that those looking for ways to stay safe were more likely to talk to a family member (69%) than to a domestic violence program (49%), doctor or nurse (34%), mental health counselor (30%), or member of the clergy (26%; Goodman, Dutton, Weinfurt, & Cook, 2003). Female friends, mothers, and sisters are especially common sources of help for survivors (Rose et al., 2000), because they often can offer practical assistance such as a place to stay, transportation to and from sources of assistance, help with the children, or even money. Equally valuable, they can provide a shoulder to cry on, advice on how to stop the abuse, encouragement for seeking outside assistance, and ideas about how to stay safe and parent effectively within the relationship. The ongoing close connections between many victims and the women in their lives mean that these supporters can tailor their interventions to match the particularized needs and strengths of a battered woman—something that advocates operating within today's service-defined framework often cannot do (Budde & Schene, 2004).

Even when a woman seeks out professional help and advice, the long-term support that is required to help her maintain safety is more likely to come from her own community (L. Kelly, 1996; Wilcox, 2000). Research suggests that a woman's access to community support can enhance her own coping skills (Arias & Pape, 1999; Heron, Twomey, Jacobs, & Kaslow, 1997; Nurius, Furrey, & Berliner, 1992) and improve her ability to successfully obtain certain kinds of formal or institutional support (Goodman, Bennett, & Dutton, 1999). For example, one study revealed that women with higher levels of social support were better able to follow through with the prosecution of their abusive partners (Goodman et al.,

1999). It appears that the stronger a woman's social support network, the less violence she experiences over time (Goodman et al., 2005). Karen, whose husband began to abuse her physically the same week they were married, credits the support of a "combination of many people over time" with helping her to leave the relationship:

> Each [person's] statement and action contributed to my ability to leave. I remember the first [coworker] in Nashville who asked me if my fat lip was caused by my [ex-husband]. He may of felt that it didn't do any good, or that he was wrong to ask. But by asking that question, it planted a seed in my mind of what was happening to me wasn't right. . . . I want to stress how terribly important the role that my [coworkers] played. True, I got support from the counselors at the abused women's shelter, but part of me felt they gave me the support because it was their job, unlike my [coworkers] who did it because they knew and cared for me. It wasn't because it was their job. I don't mean to say that the counselors weren't effective, they were. But it had even more impact on me when other people in my life gave me the same messages, that there was no excuse for my [ex-husband's] behavior, that not being happy at school, nor our financial situation, nothing gave him cause to hit me. (Family Violence Prevention Fund, 2007)

For a variety of reasons, some women lack strong social networks. Some have been isolated by their batterers; others have "used up" available support and have nowhere else to turn; and many have friends and family who do not understand or are not sympathetic to what they are going through (Kocot & Goodman, 2003; Liang, Glenn, & Goodman, 2005). As Kimberlé Crenshaw (1992) put it, "To speak, one risks the censure of one's closest allies. To remain silent renders one continually vulnerable to the kinds of abuse heaped upon people who have no voice" (p. 1472).

For all of these reasons, women's communities may serve as a critical source of strength and, simultaneously, as an obstacle to seeking help. A survivor's sense of community loyalty also may lead her to forgo outside assistance, particularly the kind that requires public testimony about the abuse or that promotes termination of the abusive relationship. A lesbian victim may worry that having her partner arrested would reinforce the idea that lesbian relationships are "deviant" or "abnormal" (Kanuha, 1990). An African American woman may be wary of racism in the system and be unwilling to contribute to the imprisonment of another Black man (Bennett, Goodman, & Dutton, 1999; Richie, 1985). A Jewish battered woman may fear tarnishing her community's image (Bograd, 1999). Although every individual woman will receive different messages and react differently to them, community pressures can have a substantial impact on the battering experience.

As a result, mainstream services can meet the needs of victims across a diversity of communities only if they (a) promote, rather than undermine, battered women's supportive community connections; (b) work to expand community leaders' capacity to help the victims living among them and to eradicate cultural and other barriers to women's safety; and (c) help survivors create new alternative sources of social support. Currently, domestic violence services typically undervalue the importance of community. Most shelters (91% in one study; Haaken & Yragui, 2003) require that women leave their own neighborhoods and use shelters in distant secret locations in the belief that doing so will keep them safer from their battering partner (Donnelly, Cook, & Wilson, 1999; Haaken & Yragui, 2003). Yet research shows that women in hidden locations are no safer during their stay than women in open shelters where community members can participate in keeping residents safe (Haaken & Yragui, 2003). In addition, for many women, relocating to a distant concealed shelter effectively severs them from their most critical sources of support and strength—including friends, religious groups, jobs, and children's school communities (Haaken & Yragui, 2003). They are thus left in the unenviable position of balancing the hope of physical safety against the potential and perhaps permanent loss of their only social support.

When women are willing to leave family and friends to reside in a shelter, they often find themselves in an alien atmosphere. Some shelter workers are not sufficiently trained to perceive or respond sensitively to cultural differences (C. C. Bell & Mattis, 2000; Donnelly et al., 2005; Schechter, 1982). Most shelters cannot afford to offer extensive services in languages other than English. The food may be strange or forbidden to members of some religious groups, and some rules may be difficult to follow for specific subgroups of women (Latta & Goodman, 2005). For example, a rule stating that residents cannot call their families for the first 72 hours of their stay cuts women off from ongoing contact with extended families and communities. This may be particularly difficult for residents of color, for whom such ties often are especially sustaining (Schechter, 1982).

Cooperation with the criminal justice system creates a similar risk of isolation from community. Immigrant women whose batterers are prosecuted, for example, may risk loss of legal status or even deportation (Jontz, 2006; Rap & Silverman, 2002). Increased exposure to law enforcement officials creates other risks as well. Survivors involved in illegal activities such as drug sales or use, whether independently or because of a batterer's coercion, may end up isolated through incarceration; as a consequence, they also may lose custody of their children.

Undermining battered women's community connections is only part of the problem. Existing services also fail to affirmatively assist those survivors who are isolated and lack any community on which to rely or those whose community members are so overburdened themselves that they have become sources of stress rather than support (Belle, 1983). The most severely battered women tend to be particularly isolated from friends and family (Goodman et al., 2005; Levendosky et al., 2004). This may be the result of a partner's abusive or coercive tactics; family or friends' repeated negative responses to their help-seeking efforts; or shame and insecurity about revealing abuse to others (Rose et al., 2000). Thus, those women in greatest need of community support often are the least able to access it.

The current service-defined responses to partner violence leave little room to help women form new social ties or repair damaged relationships. The mental health system, for example, is built on a medical model that conceptualizes women's suffering as internal. As a result, most interventions focus on changing the way women understand their own lives; they place little emphasis on ruptured social networks (Herman, 1992). Although this approach can be useful for some women, it ignores the core needs of many others. Feminist empowerment approaches, targeted at helping women discover their own ways of reconnecting with others, remain marginalized in the field and hampered by systemic obstacles. Similarly, both the criminal and civil justice systems focus heavily on separating the batterer from the victim. Virtually no attention is paid to a survivor's need to develop a support network beyond that available from short-term, system-based advocacy.

To tap battered women's communities as crucial safety and empowerment resources, service providers should make two fundamental changes. First, they need to develop a depth of cultural competence that allows and encourages a battered woman to engage in a safety planning process that is grounded in her particular community's norms and values. Cultural competence can be understood as an effort to build self-awareness about one's own privileges, stereotypes, and assumptions; to increase awareness about the populations with whom one works; and to strengthen communication skills while still prioritizing each survivor's individual experiences. As an added benefit, a deeper exploration of cultural norms and practices could facilitate entirely new, and much-needed strategies for combating domestic violence (Hamby, 2000).

Second, isolated battered women need to be given special assistance in creating new social support networks where they can engage in mutually strengthening interactions, brainstorm about coping strategies, and receive and provide emotional and practical support (L. Kelly, 1996; Smyth et al., 2006). Creating such networks could powerfully extend the reach of the anti–domestic violence movement—enabling it to embrace marginalized women and groups who are unlikely to ever access formal institutional support. As noted in a recent report of the Ms. Foundation (Das Dasgupta & Eng, 2003),

> As individuals, we are rooted within the community. For many, especially people of color, it provides the lifeblood of existence. A disempowered community weakens its members, whereas an empowered one becomes the source of their strength. A victim and her abuser live in the community and this is where the security of women inevitably rests. Even though communities may not yet be ready to support and

guarantee safety for women, the onus of ending violence begins here. (pp. 18–19)

ECONOMIC EMPOWERMENT

Poverty is profoundly intertwined with partner violence. Household income level is one of the most important overall predictors of the likelihood of partner violence against women: the lower the income, the more likely there will be violence (Bachman & Saltzman, 1995; Greenfield et al., 1998; Vest, Catlin, Chen, & Brownson, 2002). Studies consistently find that the majority of homeless women have been physically assaulted by intimate partners (Browne & Bassuk, 1997) and that more than half of all women receiving public assistance have experienced domestic violence (Lyon, 1998; Tolman & Raphael, 2000). At this point, the evidence is impossible to ignore. However, the relationship between class and partner violence is complex; poverty increases women's vulnerability to intimate abuse, and domestic violence, in turn, dramatically contributes to women's poverty (Farmer & Tiefenthaler, 2003).

Welfare recipients, for example, are particularly easy targets for abusive men (Raphael, 2000). In a recent study of women receiving welfare in Cleveland, Ohio (Scott, London, & Myers, 2002), participants described how the federally imposed, 5-year lifetime limit on welfare benefits had forced them to rely more heavily on emotionally and physically abusive partners for material help or direct financial assistance. Some extremely disadvantaged and vulnerable women "became enmeshed in even more dangerous dependencies, as they fell through public and private safety nets into drug addiction and sex work, often losing their children to the state or to their formerly abusive partners in the process" (p. 879).

Conversely, battering increases women's risk of poverty, in part through perpetrators' conscious, predictable attempts to sabotage their partners' efforts to keep a job, stay in school, obtain independent housing, or amass savings (Moe & Bell, 2004; Raphael, 2001). Bernice Hampton's story (see chap. 1, this volume), illustrates the problem: Her partner sabotaged her practical nurse training by taking her books from her and raping her before the final exam (Raphael, 2000).

As Jody Raphael (2003), the researcher largely responsible for focusing attention on the connection between poverty and battering, explained,

> The pattern is clear and repeated thousands and thousands of times on a daily basis: men use violence to keep women economically disempowered and dependent on them. Then, men manipulate these conditions of poverty to further abuse women, who are thus trapped in both poverty and abuse. (p. 368)

Women receiving public financial assistance are 10 times more likely to experience domestic violence than are other women (Tolman & Raphael, 2000). Pursuant to welfare reform requirements, these women now are required to participate in job training or welfare-to-work programs. However, their intimate partners sabotage efforts to comply by

> destroying homework assignments, keeping women up all night with arguments before key tests or job interviews, turning off alarm clocks, destroying clothing, inflicting visible facial injuries before job interviews, disabling the family car, threatening to kidnap the children from child care centers, and harassing women on the job. Threatened by the victim's potential economic independence, the abusers use violence to keep their partners at home and out of the labor market. (Raphael, 2003, p. 369)

When Linda Sexton got work as required under new Florida welfare policies, the father of her sons became increasingly abusive. Doug Pittman would come to her two jobs and embarrass her and try to get her fired:

> "I was sneaky," Pittman said. "I did a lot of things." He broke the washing machine so she wouldn't have clean clothes to wear. He hid the car keys or disconnected the car's battery and spark plugs so she couldn't get to work. He took all her money so she didn't have bus fare. He made sure he wasn't home when she needed him to take care of the kids. "I didn't want her to succeed," Pittman said. "I didn't want her to see a better life. If she sees a better life, she'll know she doesn't need me." Pittman never assaulted Sexton, but he made her fear him: "I wanted her to be afraid of me. Then I could have control over her." (Kunerth, 1997, p. A1)

Battering also pushes many women into homelessness: Across the United States, between 22% and 57% of homeless women identify partner abuse as the immediate cause (Bassuk et al., 1997; Institute for Children & Poverty, 2002; Levin, McKean, & Raphael, 2004; Wilder Research Center, 2003). More indirectly, battering can force women into a social isolation so extreme that they are cut off from family and friends who otherwise could have provided them with financial or material help (D. Coker, 2000; Raphael, 2004). Many women are evicted from their homes or denied access to housing on the basis of the crimes their abusive partners have committed against them (Lapidus, 2003). For example,

> In August, 1999, in Portland, Oregon, Tiffanie Ann Alvera's husband physically assaulted her in their government-subsidized two-bedroom apartment. The police arrested him and charged him with assault, for which he was eventually convicted. That same day, after receiving medical treatment for her injuries, Tiffanie went to court and obtained a restraining order prohibiting her husband from coming near her or into the apartment complex where they lived. When she gave the resident manager a copy of the restraining order, she was told that the management company had decided to evict her as a result of the incident. Two days later, Tiffanie's landlord served her with a termination notice, stating that she was being evicted because "you, someone in your control, or your pet, has seriously threatened immediately to inflict personal injury, or has inflicted personal injury upon the landlord or other tenants." (National Law Center on Homelessness and Poverty, 2006)

Although the Violence Against Women Act of 2005 limited some landlords' ability to engage in such revictimization of battered women, the law's protections apply only to public and some government-subsidized housing, including Section 8 vouchers and project-based housing. Women in private homes or apartments or in other forms of government-supported housing—including housing subsidized by the Low-Income Housing Tax Credit program, now the largest source of federal support for new affordable apartment construction in the country—typically remain unprotected unless local laws provide otherwise.

Finally, poverty undermines a woman's ability to benefit from mainstream interventions, such as mandatory arrest policies. Arrests appear to have a greater deterrent effect in neighborhoods where the social and legal costs of offending are high. However, these same sanctions may have the opposite effect in impoverished communities, where widely felt social exclusion both mitigates the social cost of offending and lessens its deterrent effect (National Research Council, 2004).

Despite the strong connection between poverty and domestic violence, current systemic responses pay little attention to how a woman's lack of resources can shape her experiences and needs. For example, a battered woman who seeks protection through the civil or criminal justice system is likely to miss numerous days of work to attend multiple court hearings, which may result in lost wages or even termination of employment. She may have to assume expensive extra child care during this time, and the cost of transportation to court alone may be prohibitive. Incarceration of an abusive partner also may substantially affect a victim and her children through the loss of child support, mortgage or rental assistance, or other forms of financial help. Shelters for battered women typically are designed for middle-class women in terms of the shelter climate (décor, pamphlets, reading material) as well as behavioral standards (rules for cooking, disciplining children, curfews; Donnelly et al., 2005).

Similarly, mental health providers use interventions that tend to be narrowly focused on psychological issues and ignore contextual factors such as a low-income woman's immediate (and potentially urgent) material needs. Most psychological models fail to recognize that for poor women, economic survival tends to be a top priority, with self-awareness a distant second (Coley & Beckett, 1988). As noted in chapter 3 (this volume), mental health practitioners who seek to expand their approach often are unable to access useful resources and benefits for their clients because they lack the essential training and community connections, or they are too hobbled by restrictions on what constitutes reimbursable time (Haddad & Knapp, 2000; Smyth et al., 2006). Those who do intercede might suggest a name and telephone number of a material aid program, but with the exception of some feminist therapists and others who are willing to move beyond convention, they are unlikely to put themselves in the position of actively bridging the divide between psychological and practical obstacles to safety (Grigsby & Hartman, 1997).

In addition—at least until quite recently—there has been little collaboration between the anti–domestic violence movement and obvious political allies, such as activists in the housing, labor, education, and civil rights movements, all of whom share the agenda of improving the lives of oppressed women (Das Dasgupta & Eng, 2003). The delinking of the battered women's movement from the broader feminist movement has further undermined activists' awareness of and ability to combat the relationship between poverty and violence (Coker, 2000). These links are only recently beginning to be reforged (e.g., Schneider, 2000).

The battered women's movement thus far has missed a crucial opportunity by failing to make economic empowerment a central part of its mandate. However, it is by no means too late. This issue is now subject to much discussion among anti–domestic violence activists, and new collaborations are beginning to take shape (see chap. 6, this volume).

CONCLUSION

The past 30 years have witnessed a significant increase in the resources available to victims of intimate partner abuse. But major obstacles to victim safety—consistent across the diverse fields of advocacy, mental health, and civil and criminal justice—remain. To surmount these challenges, in a serious effort to eradicate domestic violence, system actors must develop the flexibility to respond to individual women's needs, recognize the importance of survivors' relationships and social support networks, and provide a major influx of resources and assistance to those battered women struggling with the additional hurdles created by poverty.

6

Recommendations for Future Reform

Thirty years ago, intimate partner violence was considered a private matter, and efforts to help battered women were scattered and under-funded. Few local communities and no state or federal government bodies had made a real commitment to address the problem. Today, in contrast, society acknowledges and condemns violence between intimate partners. Researchers have shed light on the nature, prevalence, and con-sequences of the problem, and mental health professionals and lay advo-cates have developed practical ways to assist victims. State and federal laws now protect women through civil protection orders and punish perpetra-tors through criminal prosecutions. Community service networks and government agencies have developed social service programs that respond to survivors' needs. The rapid pace and broad scope of these changes have been truly breathtaking.

And yet, as discussed in the preceding chapters, these responses still fail to reach many battered women, the anti–domestic violence movement has strayed far from its feminist roots, and recent reforms have themselves created new, unanticipated, risks and challenges for numerous survivors. These limitations have brought the movement to an important cross-roads: Unless reform efforts can include greater flexibility and breadth, many victims will remain unsafe, and some may abandon the institutions designed to protect them.

Where do we as a society go from here? How do we bring new life to the original feminist vision of the battered women's movement?

On the basis of the critiques raised throughout this book and crystallized in chapter 5, we propose reforms that target each of the three systems analyzed here—advocacy, mental health, and justice. Our analysis is organized around the themes set out in chapter 5: voice, community, and economic empowerment. Some of the proposals are based on experiments in a handful of communities; others have not yet been implemented anywhere. Some suggestions could be put into practice fairly easily; others may seem politically infeasible at this particular moment in history. We offer this broad range of ideas to catalyze debate and activism around new approaches for ensuring battered women's physical and psychological safety.

RENEWING THE FOCUS ON WOMEN'S PARTICULAR VOICES

As discussed throughout this book, battered women who seek help from the advocacy, mental health, and justice systems are often offered (or forced to accept) services that do not fit their particular needs and may alienate them from future help-seeking efforts. For example, the advocacy system might offer only a 12-week stay in a shelter far from home; the mental health system might offer only short-term, symptom-focused psychotherapy; and the justice system might offer only separation from and prosecution of an abusive partner. Although these interventions might work well for some survivors, they are inadequate or even counterproductive for others—for example, those who wish to remain in their own communities; those who are not able or ready to separate from their abusive partners; those who are not interested in, or are unlikely to benefit from, traditional short-term psychotherapy; and those who are in desperate need of financial assistance. The recommendations that follow are designed to promote the voices of these underserved battered women, without sacrificing the substantial gains of the past 30 years.

Advocacy

Resurrecting a survivor-defined approach to battered women's advocacy will require significant change in private and public service agencies. Such change is only realistic with the support of foundations and government funders.

First, funders and policymakers must give advocates the flexibility and resources to assist a far wider range of women than is currently permitted, including survivors who are substance abusers, homeless, seriously mentally ill, unwilling to leave their own communities, or interested in maintaining their ties with an abusive partner. Women who themselves have used violence in their relationships or who otherwise do not fit the classic image of a helpless victim also should be eligible for services. In addition, broader eligibility criteria should be complemented by broader goals for survivors with multiple and complex needs. These women need to be given the autonomy to formulate their own priorities (in consultation with a well-trained advocate) and to receive individualized assistance. An addicted victim may or may not have sobriety as her primary goal; a homeless victim may or may not choose stable housing as her first focus (Smyth, Goodman, & Glenn, 2006).

Second, domestic violence programs should adopt broader measures of their own effectiveness. Outcome measures need to be multiple rather than binary, and definitions of success should be flexible rather than rigid. Indicators of progress might encompass outcomes as diverse as achieving a safer relationship with an abusive partner, engaging more deeply with potentially supportive friends and family members, articulating more clearly a set of short and long-term safety goals and taking several steps toward attaining them, moving from the streets to a shelter, obtaining employment, or developing a concrete safety plan. Funders must support the use of these flexible nuanced definitions of success rather than the limited ones they currently impose on their grantees (Bonisteel & Green, 2005; Smyth et al., 2006) so that advocates can expand their work to fit the needs of a broader population of women.

Third, to gain a full understanding of survivors' goals, advocates must continue to learn about the cultural, religious, class, and ethnic communities that comprise their client base. Advocates educated in this way will be better able to help victims assert their needs and will be able to listen and respond in more meaningful ways. Hiring bilingual staff and advocates who come from the communities they serve is a critical step forward. Even where hiring diversity is not possible, staff members need to ensure that they are working toward cultural sensitivity. Such efforts require training and ongoing self-monitoring, particularly as to how an advocate's own biases may be affecting her work (Bent-Goodley, 2004; Kasturirangan, Krishnan, & Riger, 2004). In addition, shelters need sufficient funding to more consistently provide participants with access to familiar food, rituals, cultural symbols, and forms of socializing. Shelter rules for cooking, disciplining children, and curfews need to be culturally consistent or—better yet—developed by community members themselves (Donnelly, Cook, Van Ausdale, & Foley, 2005). Such efforts would promote a sense of unity and support that is crucial for battered women during a postcrisis shelter stay.

Finally, advocates need sufficient autonomy to help a woman fulfill her individual goals, even if those goals conflict with those of the agency for which the advocate works. For example, an advocate who works within a district attorney's office should retain the flexibility to provide services to any survivor, even one who opposes criminal prosecution of her abusive partner. The advocate needs to ensure that every woman fully appreciates the potential advantages and disadvantages of refusing to cooperate with the government but also should be free to provide survivors with meaningful advocacy, regardless of the impact on the prosecution. In addition, advocates should be able to maintain confidentiality (at least to the extent that this is possible without exposing others, particularly children, to physical harm), even if this practice conflicts with the agency's usual reporting standards. Such victim-centered advocacy may only be possible if advocates work in prosecutors' offices but are employed by, and report to, private domestic violence organizations.

Mental Health System

A more woman-defined approach within the mental health system also would require numerous changes. Researchers and mental health service providers have made great strides toward developing sensitive interventions for victims of intimate partner violence, particularly those with posttraumatic stress disorder (Abel, 2000; Chalk & King, 1998; Lundy & Grossman, 2001), but much remains to be done.

Most important, mainstream mental health service providers need to expand their focus to include the full range of external obstacles to battered women's safety, such as lack of transportation, residential instability, insufficient information about battering and available community resources, lack of physical or cultural access to domestic violence services, insufficient financial resources, inadequate police or other criminal justice responses, and immigration difficulties (Sharma, 2001). Although feminist therapy theorists have made substantial efforts to incorporate these issues into their work, many practitioners, hampered by a range of systemic factors, do not go far enough in addressing them.

We are not suggesting that a mental health worker's job description should become interchangeable with that of an advocate. But collaboration should become the norm. Therapists can bring to the table their in-depth understanding of the mental and emotional impact of a woman's traumatic experience; advocates can bring their broader and deeper experience with helping women address external obstacles (Briere & Jordan, 2004; Warshaw & Moroney, 2002). Some of this collaboration may occur through cross-training, coalition building, and system-level coordination, but communication and collaboration around the cases of individual women is also critical. Case-specific communication can be facilitated by interdisciplinary hiring practices and by enabling advocates and mental health providers to work together within government agencies and private organizations. Such collaboration may require mental health professionals to sacrifice their long-cherished status in the social service system hierarchy to make room for advocates as coequals.

In addition to developing new methods of practice, feminist therapists and other mental health services providers need to find new places to practice. Far too often, therapists are unwilling to leave the confines of their offices to do outreach, let alone to practice their work, in those spaces battered women actually frequent. Greater outreach would increase victims' access to services as well as provide cover for those who fear their batterer's anger or the stigma of seeking mental health services. Many batterers will not permit their partners to seek mental health counseling, but they might be willing to allow them to attend a "women only" night at the local church or hair salon. If mental health professionals demonstrate their willingness to go wherever it is necessary and to learn about, and be respectful of, a broader range of cultural norms and practices, then many more women are likely to feel more comfortable entering therapy.

However, therapists cannot develop this kind of flexibility in the absence of at least two fundamental systemic changes. First, reimbursement policies under managed care must change radically to ensure that domestic violence survivors receive the services they need (see chap. 3, this volume). Practitioners need to be able to work with women in a context that does not require the imposition of pathologizing diagnoses. Also, although the reigning paradigm of brief psychotherapy works well for some, insurance policies also must cover longer term interventions for women who need "time to build trust, time to take the risk of disclosing often humiliating abuse, time to explore options, time to begin implementing a plan of action to escape abuse, and time to begin and complete the exhausting healing process" (Grigsby & Hartman, 1997, p. 489). In addition, to enable practitioners to assist women with needs outside of the therapy office, insurers must permit reimbursement for time in excess of the traditional 45- to 50-minute therapeutic hour (Gomez & Yassen, 2007).

Second, new methods need to be accepted for evaluating mental health interventions (see chap. 3, this volume). In the current managed care climate, controlled studies are the gold standard for treatment and reimbursement. However, when proof of a specific intervention's success rests on simple outcome metrics, such as a reduction in a specific set of predetermined symptoms, the result may be a deemphasis on, and a devaluation of, interventions that promote changes that are not easily measurable or that do not match traditional notions of success (Smyth et al., 2006). Though quantitative empirical analyses based on narrow outcome measures have an important place in the armament of useful evaluation methodologies, participatory and qualitative methods also are legitimate tools. What Laura S. Brown (2005) has written about feminist therapists is broadly applicable: "Feminist therapists value data from randomized controlled clinical trials—and we also value evidence arising from qualitative studies, from clinical examples, and from the consumers of our services" (p. 9). Such alternative methods are particularly well suited to feminist therapy approaches that are open-ended in terms of length and goals.

Transformation of the managed care system will not occur overnight. As scholar and advocate John D. Norcross (2005) has written,

> What would it take to transform our voices of dissent into widespread changes in insurance reimbursement, health policy, and more humane societal values? Ten times the money, the fervor, the professional commitment currently being expended. . . . We would need to mobilize on the order of magnitude of physicians who are successfully lobbying for malpractice limits and tort reform, and of gun control opponents who, despite public opinion and scientific research to the contrary, are able to effectively stymie progressive legislation. (p. 153)

This is a tall order, but success is not impossible. Efforts to humanize the mental health system will be strengthened by the support of researchers and practitioners who work with battered women.

Finally, many service providers remain unaware of how to identify abuse victims in their practice or how to work with those who self-identify. Graduate programs in psychology, psychiatry, and social work should consider including mandatory training in partner violence screening and therapy. Education and training should include opportunities for clinicians to explore how cultural forces affect their approach to therapy, as well as their clients' experiences (American Psychological Association, 2003; Gomez & Yassen, 2007; D. W. Sue & Sue, 2003).

Awareness alone is not enough. Listening to survivors also means translating cultural sensitivity into concrete improvements in mental health services (Hwang, 2006). New interventions should be specifically targeted to diverse populations of domestic violence survivors, including new immigrants; ethnic, racial, and religious minorities who were born in the United States; lesbian, bisexual, and transgender populations; and poor women.

Justice System

The justice system needs to undergo substantial change before it can meaningfully accommodate the needs of individual women. Although mandatory arrest laws and no-drop prosecution policies were adopted in part to promote battered women's safety, these policies tend to be applied rigidly, even where they may expose women to more rather than less violence. The solution is greater flexibility: Police and prosecutors should have limited authority to decide, in collaboration with victims, whether arrest and prosecution make sense given their particular circumstances.

Prosecutors could take one step in this direction by seriously considering a victim's request that the office decline to pursue a criminal case, even where it formally merits prosecution. In some cases there are strong indicators that the prosecution itself will create a high risk of severe batterer retaliation against a victim (e.g., Dugan, Nagin, & Rosenfeld, 2001), but for a variety of reasons there is little likelihood that the court will impose a lengthy jail sentence. A prosecutor should consider prioritizing long-term victim safety over offender accountability, even if this means dropping charges.

Prosecutors tend to react to this recommendation with extreme discomfort. Even if they recognize that a conviction is unlikely to protect the victim in the long run, and may even increase her risk of future harm, their primary responsibility is to ensure offender accountability, and it is personally and politically difficult to depart from convention. This is particularly true when there is no guarantee that a different approach—intensive advocacy alone, for example—will ensure the victim's safety. When faced with the risk that a victim will be reabused, most prosecutors take comfort in remaining within the professional norm. However, if the state is to embrace a more meaningful strategy for eradicating domestic violence, other options must remain on the table.

The suggestion that the government occasionally refrain from prosecution is in no way meant to endorse a return to the lax prosecutorial practices of an earlier era. Prosecutors must not cede control over the criminal justice system to abusers who can threaten or beat their partners into requesting that charges be dropped. Instead, prosecutors must confine this option to cases in which the victim requests it and the facts support an assessment that dropping charges will promote the victim's long-term safety.[1] In addition, district attorney's offices must provide battered women with intensive advocacy services to ensure both that a survivor is making her own decision, independent of the perpetrator's coercion, and that she will be in a better position to access resources if any future violence does occur. Until substantially expanded and woman-centered advocacy is available to survivors within the criminal justice system, this proposal will be too high risk to implement and must remain a hope for the future.

Another, less radical, way to increase flexibility is for the government to consider postponing prosecution in some cases. Prosecutors could accumulate the evidence necessary to go forward but delay filing charges while the victim receives the advocacy services she needs to take action or to move beyond the batterer's psychological control and to assess her situation with greater clarity.

Increased communication is another important area for reform. For prosecutors to choose a course that will best serve a battered woman, they need to have all pertinent information at their disposal at the initial charging stage. In reality, they typically have limited time to devote to an individual case, especially at the outset, and thus tend to focus on the most recent incident of violence. Prosecutors often are unaware of any history of violence the victim has suffered at the hands of her abusive partner (Epstein, Bell, & Goodman, 2003), whereas private advocates and civil attorneys tend to focus far more time and attention on past incidents of abuse. By creating opportunities for advocates, attorneys, and survivors themselves to share such information, prosecutors may be able to add charges that otherwise never would have been brought. These additional charges may increase the length of a jail sentence for the perpetrator, giving the victim additional time and space to create a new, safer life. Or, when appropriate, such discussions could result in a prosecutor agreeing to decline pursuit of certain charges when doing so would increase the victim's sense of support and general willingness to coop-

---

[1] What any individual batterer will do can never be predicted with certainty, and therefore one can never be sure of what will best ensure the victim's long-term safety. There is much debate over the use of risk-assessment instruments that attempt to predict what an individual will do on the basis of similarities between that person and others in a database where outcomes are known (e.g., Hart, Cooke, & Michie, 2006; Litwack, 2001). Although the details of this debate are beyond the scope of this chapter, it seems clear that predictions that work well in the aggregate are not necessarily applicable to an individual case. Complex and dynamic circumstances distinguish every incident and potential future incident of violence. If an advocate can work closely with a survivor to understand and address these complexities, the survivor stands the best chance of achieving safety (Bennett Cattaneo & Goodman, 2007).

erate. Such collaboration may not be realistic unless and until reliable research can demonstrate that it has beneficial effects, such as a reduction in recidivist violence (for an example of one such collaboration, see Epstein et al., 2003).

In both the criminal and civil justice systems, community responses must go far beyond the current focus on coordinated initiation of cases (through such means as a domestic violence intake center, where a victim can obtain "one-stop shopping" access to civil and criminal justice system advocates) or coordinated logistics of cases (through such means as a unified domestic violence court, where civil protection order and criminal prosecution cases may be scheduled for the same date before the same judge). Meaningful coordination requires that all providers who respond to a particular woman fully understand her needs and concerns. Service providers, including the prosecution, must routinely share case-specific information and even case-specific goals across agencies and providers to respond successfully to a client's needs. Although professional client confidentiality requirements impose limits on information exchange, far greater collaboration is possible; indeed, virtually no such case-specific collaboration currently occurs (one exception is described in Epstein et al., 2003).

Finally, coordinated community responses must be structured so that lay advocates are encouraged to assert their perspectives. Because they are often the people who spend the most time in direct contact with survivors, they are typically in the best position to understand and communicate a victim's needs and wishes. However, their meaningful participation in criminal justice system collaborations are currently curtailed by a cultural climate in which the views of legal professionals predominate. A new atmosphere, in which state actors understand and value advocates' perspectives, may not be realistic in the short term. One step toward reaching this goal would be for research to demonstrate positive outcomes for such an approach in terms of victim safety and perpetrator accountability (Epstein et al., 2003).

RESTORING SUPPORTIVE COMMUNITIES AND CREATING NEW ONES

As discussed in previous chapters, current practice fails to incorporate essential community building for battered women. Programs are not as responsive to women who decide to remain with their partners as they are to those who wish to leave. Service providers rarely make active efforts to create new social networks that might support battered women and provide long-term reinforcement of their efforts to remain safe. Far more needs to be done both to help survivors reconnect with family and friends from whom they have become isolated and to educate communities about ways to assist victims.

Advocacy

Public and private funders need to support advocates in their efforts to further develop the resources available to battered women who are not ready to leave their partners. Any decision to stay in an abusive relationship should be an informed one, and it may take time to help a woman understand and consider the full range of options available to her. This may be particularly true for battered women in intimate terrorism relationships in which, long after the violence stops, a batterer's psychological control may continue to impede a victim's ability to imagine a safer life. Regardless of the services and time available, some survivors will decide to remain with their partners, at least in the short term (see chap. 5, this volume). These women need advocacy and support so that they can exercise this choice as safely as possible. Advocacy programs and the funders who support them need to shift their focus from "How can we help her leave?" to "How can we help her gain a realistic degree of safety right now, as well as in the future?" Although most advocates already use safety planning and danger assessment to assist women who stay with their partners, new supplemental strategies are needed. As one example, advocates could routinely reach out to members of a battered woman's social network and enlist their support for her efforts to stay safe within the relationship (Burstow, 1992; L. Kelly, 1996; Peled, Eisikovitz, Enosh, & Winstok, 2000).

Advocacy programs also need to ensure that survivors can obtain assistance without sacrificing community ties. To some extent, in some locations, this goal can be accomplished by building shelter spaces in the geographic and cultural communities where clients reside. Despite conventional arguments in favor of secret shelter locations, such as their importance in ensuring resident and staff security, there is no evidence that concealment actually promotes safety. Indeed, as previously discussed, separating women from their communities can be quite harmful (Haaken & Yragui, 2003). Some activists are now challenging the prevailing practice, arguing that only community-based shelters can offer battered women the chance to remain connected with people who can provide them with long-term support, help them build new lives that remain rooted in what was good about their old ones, and address the myriad issues that could prevent them from exiting a battering relationship (Haaken & Yragui, 2003). In addition, when shelters are open, a community can develop a sense of ownership of the problem of domestic violence and see its own role in creating a solution (Haaken & Yragui, 2003). In the words of one activist (Tyra Lindquist, Washington State Coalition Against Domestic Violence),

> The advantages [of shelter locations being public] are reaped primarily by programs that use [the information] positively as public education and support. It's an opportunity to make domestic violence apparent as a problem. People drive by it every day and can see that [the rate of] domestic violence is not going down when the shelter is always full. Neighbors watching out can keep the shelter safe. The shelter needs to build relationships with business and neighbors and educate them as to how to respond when they see something amiss. It's being in people's faces about it. (quoted in Haaken & Yragui, 2003, p. 60)

Despite these advantages, many communities will not welcome shelters into their neighborhoods right away. In these areas, shelter workers can begin to develop relationships with community leaders and activists to establish a dialogue that may gradually lead to acceptance.

But helping battered women reconnect with existing communities is not enough. Advocates also need to focus on developing new, safe social networks for women who do not have them. Peer support groups are one important tool in this endeavor. Successful peer support programs have been created in locations as varied as domestic violence shelters; public housing developments; hair braiding salons; and churches, mosques, and synagogues. Some focus discussion directly on the experience of abuse; others focus primarily on parenting, self-care, or other issues that participants find more pressing. Given both the stigma of domestic violence and the prioritization of needs in some communities, a substantial number of women are far more likely to attend a group that aims to help them mother their children more effectively than one that focuses exclusively on the impact of partner violence (Latta & Goodman, 2005).

Finally, advocates need to reach out to community leaders in religious institutions, health care agencies, educational institutions, workplaces, and other community settings to transform these places into supportive environments for battered women. Community leaders could help bring women together to support each other, work toward political change, and develop new paths toward collective empowerment. Scholar and activist William Oliver (2000) has highlighted the importance of African American churches and radio stations as venues for community education about domestic violence. In Boston, for example, advocates run an interfaith program to train clergy and congregants about the dynamics of domestic violence, about how to implement safe and appropriate prevention and intervention strategies, and about local domestic violence services (Safe Havens Interfaith Partnership Against Domestic Violence, 2002). Because the trainings involve both clergy and lay leaders, the information is disseminated through various channels, both from the pulpit and in informal conversations during church social hours (Latta & Goodman, 2005). Similar programs might be useful in communities across the country.

Mental Health System

Peer support or empowerment groups have been the chief vehicles used by mental health practitioners to help domestic violence victims reengage with others. Currently, these groups are typically facilitated by professionals and hold their meetings in the offices of domestic violence agencies or at community mental health centers. Providers could substantially expand the reach of these programs in several ways. For example, mental health professionals could promote access for women who are unlikely to enter a traditional mental health setting by contacting small business owners and offering to host a series of informal discussions about domestic violence during a lunch break or by facilitating a group at a local nail salon. They also could enhance access across cultural groups by creating discussion groups for students who are taking classes in citizenship or English as a second language (Kim, 2002).

These and other similar innovations are realistic only if mental health providers can reduce their reliance on insurance companies with restrictive reimbursement policies (see chap. 5, this volume). Moreover, for such projects to succeed, practitioners need to develop sustained relationships with community members so that in the long run, they can step back and support others in organizing and developing their own methods for building social support.

Justice System

In the civil justice system, promoting community building will require an overhaul of the current reflexive judicial bias in favor of partner separation. Judicial training is one path toward alleviating this problem, but many judges are not particularly receptive to advocacy-based training programs (Epstein, 1999). Solid research that compares the psychological and physical security of battered women who choose to stay and those who are forced to leave against their will could be extraordinarily useful in any project designed to expand judicial perspectives. As noted previously, judges also tend to prefer joint custody awards in partner abuse cases; additional research and training on the risks battered women face when forced to maintain contact with abusive fathers is needed here as well.

It is also crucial to develop viable alternatives or supplements to the justice system. One of the most promising of these is the family group conference, a specialized model within the broader—and controversial— restorative justice movement. Restorative justice represents a departure from the traditional criminal justice focus on offender accountability, emphasizing instead hearing, restoring, and empowering individual victims and their larger communities and doing so in a way consistent with the survivor's culture and context (Daly & Stubbs, 2006). Typically, restorative justice models are participatory processes that center on a meeting of the accused offender, the victim, community supporters, and a facilitator. Maximizing the active involvement of all involved parties is a key part of this process. The participants work together to agree on a way for the offender to make up for his wrongdoing, including apologizing and making some sort of reparations (D. Coker, 2004; Curtis-Fawley & Daly, 2005; Grauwiler & Mills, 2004; Stubbs, 2004; Zehr, 2004). This process may occur in conjunction with, or independent of, the criminal justice system.

Many battered women's advocates have expressed deep reservations about applying restorative justice models in intimate partner violence cases. As critics have pointed out, many of the advantages of restorative justice are inapplicable or even counterindicated in domestic violence cases. First, restorative justice practices tend to focus on a discrete past event for which the perpetrator can express regret and make amends. In theory, this will prevent society from pathologizing the perpetrator and will allow him to move on. However, in the partner abuse context, violence typically recurs, and an apology is simply a part of the cyclical nature of the relationship dynamic; further, society tends to tolerate rather than pathologize this form of violence. Second, victims report that an advantage of restorative justice is the opportunity to get to know the perpetrator as a human being and to understand that they were targeted randomly. These factors do not apply to domestic violence cases, where victims are intimately connected with their abusive partners. Finally, restorative justice models are based on the assumption that victims can assert their own interests in a mediation process that involves the perpetrator. Successful mediation requires relatively equal bargaining power between the parties, as well as the ability to exercise free choice, but as discussed throughout this book, those assumptions rarely apply in partner violence settings (Curtis-Fawley & Daly, 2005; Stubbs, 2002).

Given the scope and seriousness of these concerns, work in this area must proceed with caution. The bulk of the advocacy community's hesitation, however, turns on the perpetrator's role as an active participant in most restorative justice processes. This concern is somewhat less salient in the family group conferencing model, where the batterer's participation is optional.

The family group conferencing model was pioneered in New Zealand and has been used in association with child welfare, adult probation, and parole cases in Canada and the United States (Pennell & Francis, 2005).[2] In cases that involve domestic violence, the family group conference brings together the survivor, her family members, and other close supporters to form a "family group" that establishes a plan for addressing the violence. The goal is to "overcome the isolation of survivors, acknowledge women and children's continued connections with the batterer and his family, and provide avenues for abusers to take public responsibility for their actions" (Pennell & Francis, 2005, p. 677). The conference allows the family to obtain support from community members and state actors as a supplement to a more formal court or government agency proceeding.

A conference coordinator works intensively with family members to ensure that they can participate in a safe, effective, and culturally consistent way. They typically spend close to 30 hours to prepare for a single meeting, focusing in particular on making certain the victim will feel sufficiently safe to voice her concerns (Pennell, 2006; Pennell & Burford, 2002). Conferences are held in a community setting to which transportation is provided, with chairs in a circle and familiar food. Interpreters are provided when necessary. Any family members who feel at risk are encouraged to bring a support person with them. During the conference, the coordinator first summarizes the family's history and the concerns to be addressed, and representatives from community agencies provide information about potential resources available to the family. After this presentation, the coordinator and community agency representatives leave, and the family group formulates its own plan to address the violence and any other issues of concern and establishes a monitoring and evaluation process. Before the plan goes into effect, it must be approved by the referring agency, and that agency continues to monitor

---

[2] Many families referred for child-related issues bring adult domestic violence concerns to the table as well, and in some sites in Canada, domestic violence cases have been referred directly by government agencies. In one study of 32 Canadian families referred from child welfare, adult parole or probation, and youth corrections, family group conferencing coordinators documented the presence of an adult abusing an adult in 21 of the families, with nearly all of the violence committed by men against women (Pennell & Burford, 2000, 2002).

the case.[3] In cases that occur in conjunction with a court proceeding, the plan can be incorporated into a judicial order, with a subsequent date set for an implementation review (Joan Pennell, personal communication, December 11, 2006).[4] Occasionally, the abusive partner participates in the conference. If this does not appear to be a safe course of action, however, family members may participate in his stead (Pennell, 2005).

Although more research is needed to assess the efficacy and safety of this model, initial data from 28 Canadian families show positive results. Researchers conducted 12- and 24-month follow-up interviews with these families and compared them with a control group.[5] Participants were asked about a series of domestic violence indicators, such as "mother exhibits fear and anxiety in presence of her partner." Those who participated in the family group conferences reported 84 of these indicators as present before the conference and only 34 during the 12- to 24-month postconference follow-up period. In contrast, control group families reported a change from 45 to 52 (Pennell, 2005; Pennell & Burford, 2000). These results are preliminary; it is possible, however, that additional data collected over the longer term may serve to assuage advocates' concerns with this model. If so, family group conferencing may provide a useful model for deepening the role of community in battered women's efforts to address the violence in their lives.

INCREASING OPPORTUNITIES
FOR ECONOMIC EMPOWERMENT

Although domestic violence cuts across class lines, poverty plays a significant role in the occurrence of domestic violence and places powerful limits on battered women's options for safety and escape (see chap. 5, this volume). Financial control is a powerful form of abuse within a violent relationship, and where a victim is financially dependent on her abuser, leaving the relationship may well mean starting over with, quite literally,

---

[3] Monitoring systems remain underdeveloped in family group conferencing. Until such systems are firmly established, this model cannot be disconnected from criminal justice oversight.

[4] Joan Pennell is a professor in the Department of Social Work at North Carolina State University, Raleigh.

[5] Although an attempt was made to match the two groups, this was difficult because families referred for conferencing appeared to face more serious difficulties.

nothing. The employment-related effects of domestic violence—in the form of depressed wages due to diminished job performance, lost jobs, and missed opportunities for education and other forms of advancement—can long outlast the violence itself (Farmer & Tiefenthaler, 2004). Simultaneously, macroeconomic pressures affecting all women impose additional barriers to longer term economic security for survivors. The gender wage gap is one example of such a hurdle: In 2002, women as a group were paid only approximately 76% of what men were paid for full-time, year-round work (Caiazza, Shaw, & Werschkul, 2004).[6]

Despite the crucial impact of money on the lives and options of battered women, until quite recently little attention has been paid to formulating a coherent policy agenda for survivors' economic empowerment (Economic Stability Working Group, 2002). The necessity of meeting survivors' economic needs has been thrown into sharp relief through changes in federal and state government antipoverty measures over the past decade. These changes include welfare reform, which substantially reduced the social safety net for many poor women (Correia & VonDeLinde, 2002).

To fully address the economic effects of intimate partner violence, government and private entities must respond to victims' immediate and longer term needs (Correia & VonDeLinde, 2002; Farmer & Tiefenthaler, 2003). As the following discussion suggests, responsive policies and practices should range from highly targeted interventions to broad economic and employment policy decisions that empower women generally and poor battered women in particular.

Advocacy

Advocates have begun increasing their efforts to directly address the economic needs of poor women who are exposed to domestic violence (Pyles, 2006; Raphael & Shapiro, 2002). New, creative programs have been imple-

---

[6] The wage gap is worse for African American, Latina, and Native American women. In 1999, median annual earnings for White women who were working full time and year round were at 70% of those of White men, whereas African American, Latina, and Native American women were at 62.5%, 52.5%, and 57.8%, respectively (Caiazza et al., 2004).

mented in a small number of jurisdictions; many more may soon be put into practice.

Short-Term Assistance

Advocates have begun to pursue a wide range of strategies to provide survivors with immediate financial relief. One crucial source of emergency assistance is direct cash disbursements; even a small amount can be sufficient to alleviate the economic crises that often accompany a woman's transition out of an abusive relationship. Advocates have convinced some state governments to devise flexible, one-time cash assistance programs. Massachusetts, for example, targets its program to reduce the needs of survivors in transition, providing money for expenses such as security deposits on rental homes (Economic Stability Working Group, 2002).

Advocates also have persuaded private funders to provide flexible "bridge funds" to assist victims transitioning out of violent relationships (N. Otero, personal communication, January 25, 2007). In addition, they have convinced a number of private employers to establish policies that support the provision of short-term loans, pay advances, and vacation time payouts for victims in crisis (Economic Stability Working Group, 2002; see also http://www.safeatworkcoalition.org). Levi Strauss & Co., for example, has provided such support to employees who are struggling with domestic violence, as well as to employees facing other emergency financial needs, through its Red Tab Foundation (Sachs, 1999). Other advocates are working to convince banks to adopt policies to protect jointly held accounts against unilateral closure, to notify joint account holders of suspicious activity, and to permit victims to freeze assets (Economic Stability Working Group, 2002). Similar innovations are needed in communities across the country.

Workplace flexibility policies also are critical for survivors who are attempting to move toward independence from their abusers. These policies help battered women maintain full-time employment while they handle time-consuming transitional issues such as attending court proceedings, managing transitional child care, or searching for an alternate place to live (Bardasi & Gornick, 2003). A handful of businesses currently permit flexible leave for such purposes, and advocates across the country are using these policies as models in an effort to persuade other employers to do the same (NOW Legal Defense and Education Fund, 2002; see also http://www.safeatworkcoalition.org).

Longer Term Assistance

Battered women's economic empowerment also requires longer term support. Like poor women generally, low-income domestic violence survivors typically lack access to programs that could enable them to obtain sustainable employment, housing, welfare, child support, and asset protection.

Perhaps the most crucial source of financial stability is full-time sustainable employment. Advocates in some states have encouraged emergency shelters to discontinue policies that prohibit or discourage residents from working; unless working puts the survivor in greater danger, transitional services should facilitate economic stability through employment (Economic Stability Working Group, 2002).

Increased employer sensitization to domestic violence issues is another important strategy. Advocates have convinced some employers to establish written policies that relate to domestic violence; to expand employee assistance programs to provide concrete support to victims of intimate partner abuse, including help in obtaining protection orders; and to train managers to identify possible abusive situations and handle them sensitively and lawfully (Economic Stability Working Group, 2002; NOW Legal Defense and Education Fund, 2002). Liz Claiborne, Inc., has been a leader in this area through its "Love Is Not Abuse" program, which includes both progressive internal policy and corporate philanthropy in the areas of family and dating violence.

Because housing typically is the single largest item in a family's budget (U.S. Department of Labor, 2004), access to it is crucial to a victim's fiscal survival. Advocates successfully ensured that the Violence Against Women Act of 2005 prohibited discrimination against domestic violence victims in public and federally subsidized housing; the law also permitted "lease bifurcation," so that a public landlord may evict an offender tenant while permitting a victim tenant to remain. Advocates around the country need to educate survivors about these rights and to follow the example of several states that have adopted similar laws prohibiting eviction discrimination against victims by all landlords (e.g., Colorado Security Deposit Act, 2006; Rhode Island Fair Housing Practice Act, 2006). Recent amendments to Washington, DC's law go further and bar various forms of discrimination in private, public, and subsidized housing against victims (The Protection from Discriminatory Eviction for Victims of Domestic Violence Amendment Act, 2006).

In addition, advocates in some states have developed programs to help survivors clean up credit or housing histories that can make it difficult to rent in the private market. On a national level, advocacy groups are pressing the federal government to create housing voucher programs that would prioritize victims of intimate partner violence and provide housing search support so that the often onerous search for qualifying housing does not interfere with survivors' employment or other economically stabilizing activities.[7]

Victims often depend on welfare to provide the economic wherewithal to leave a violent relationship (California Institute of Mental Health, 2000; Raphael, 2000). The federal welfare system includes a Family Violence Option (FVO), which permits, but does not require, states to waive existing time restrictions and work requirements for recipients who are coping with domestic violence. Advocates across the country are hoping to make the FVO mandatory. In states already providing relief under the FVO, advocates are pushing to improve delivery of its benefits by creating more effective domestic violence screening and by reducing caseworker discretion in denying waivers (Lindhorst & Padgett, 2005). The advocacy community could play a central role in persuading legislatures to create similar waivers for food stamp programs, which provide additional income support for many survivors and their families (Economic Stability Working Group, 2002).

Another key to a battered woman's economic independence is the availability of child support that is paid regularly and through a process that does not expose a survivor or her children to further violence. In sev-

---

[7] The organizations that have advocated for housing authorities to adopt such preferences or start such programs include the National Housing Law Project, the National Law Center on Homelessness and Poverty, BayLegal (Bay Area Legal Aid), and Ohio State Legal Services.

eral states, advocates have ensured that their laws authorize child support awards in protection orders and that their court systems prioritize child support hearings where there are allegations of partner abuse, apply local child support guidelines consistently, and issue sanctions when abusers do not meet their payment obligations (see Epstein, 1999). Battered women's advocates in a growing number of states also are working with employers to ensure prompt compliance with court-ordered wage garnishment to meet child support obligations for victims (Economic Stability Working Group, 2002).

Advocates also need to continue initial efforts to sensitize the financial industry about money-related partner abuse and about its long-term effects on victims. Banks and other financial institutions could institute policies to protect joint accounts from abuse by one partner, educate customers, and develop programs to help survivors open bank accounts and restore damaged credit. Convincing government agencies to provide incentives for such programs could be a much-needed catalyst in this area (Economic Stability Working Group, 2002).

Finally, efforts to develop opportunities for battered women's economic advancement cannot fully succeed unless they are part of a broader movement to address women's poverty. If advocates work toward improved conditions for domestic violence victims without coordinating their efforts with other entities, they will lose the concentrated power that collaboration can provide. Coalitions working toward improvements in poverty, housing, education, rights for the disabled, welfare, and labor rights are key allies (Schechter, 1982). As one example, anti–domestic violence advocates are now collaborating with antipoverty activists to implement living-wage legislation; because women are disproportionately represented in low-wage jobs, raising the minimum rate of pay would enable more survivors to leave abusive partners on whom they are financially dependent (Sklar, Mykyta, & Wefald, 2001).

Of course, different policy packages will be appropriate for different communities, because prevailing economic conditions vary widely (Benson & Fox, 2004; Correia & VonDeLinde, 2002). What works to provide economic stability to a survivor in rural Iowa may not be effective for a woman in Boston or San Francisco. The key is recognition that both individualized and systemic policy interventions are needed to address the immediate and longer term effects of intimate partner violence.

Mental Health System

Mental health treatment for poor clients in general and for low-income domestic violence victims in particular has received far too little attention in the general psychotherapy literature (Lott, 2002; L. Smith, 2005; for a notable exception, see Miranda et al., 2006). When poverty has been discussed, it is often to point out that poor people tend to drop out of treatment prematurely or are unable to benefit from what therapists have to offer (S. Sue & Lam, 2002). Mental health theorists and practitioners need to focus more concretely on the fact that for many battered women, violence and its psychological effects are sometimes secondary to the experience of economic oppression and, conversely, that survivors' ability to advance their economic self-sufficiency may be severely compromised by posttraumatic stress disorder, depression, or the other mental health issues that accompany abuse (Herman, 1992). More research and theorizing is needed to develop mental health interventions that incorporate the psychological impact of survivors' economic oppression, the ways in which poverty shapes the experience of victimization, and how financial security can enhance a victim's sense of dignity and connection to the world.

Because the obstacles to economic empowerment may be both psychological and practical, therapists must stretch beyond their traditional role and offer victims concrete assistance toward greater financial self-sufficiency (Smyth et al., 2006). To accomplish this goal, therapists need to collaborate closely with advocates and others who can work more directly with women on economic security issues. Such work should go beyond simply making referral calls on a client's behalf. Feminist therapists have demonstrated the power of developing strong relationships with service providers in relevant agencies and closely monitoring the advocacy work that goes on outside the therapy office.

Justice System

Historically, there has been little connection between the justice system and the economic empowerment of litigants. In domestic violence cases, a victim may be informed about the possibility that she is eligible for a limited amount of state assistance through crime victims' compensation funds, and she may be referred to community agencies for assistance with welfare, food stamps, and housing. However, given the large numbers of victims who use the courts in their efforts to escape intimate partner abuse, far more substantial links with antipoverty resources are needed.

Initial steps have been made in a handful of states to link civil protection order and longer term child support cases, thus increasing the likelihood that a parent survivor will receive at least one form of relatively long-term economic assistance (Epstein, 1999). Case coordination is crucial because it reduces a batterer's ability to avoid a child support obligation through intimidation tactics, such as threatening a custodial parent victim with violence, kidnapping the children, or filing fabricated child abuse reports against her. Court-based collection systems are most effective when they protect confidential information, including a victim's identity and location. Additional justice system efforts might include the provision of sufficient resources to support a survivor's interactions with the court, including funds for transportation, quality child care, and compensation for work days missed because of court hearings.

CONCLUSION

Over the past 30 years, our society has revolutionized its response to battered women. Far more is now known about the nature and scope of intimate partner violence. Advocates have successfully raised public awareness of the problem and mobilized the political will to intervene. They have created hotlines and shelters and have partnered with the government to expand the resources available to survivors. Mental health providers have developed theories that are increasingly able to explain the symptoms exhibited by victims, as well as therapeutic practices that can help survivors to cope. Activists, police, prosecutors, and judges have greatly expanded battered women's access to the criminal and civil justice systems, and many battered women are now able to benefit from the wide range of protections these systems can provide.

But numerous obstacles to survivors' safety still remain, and reform efforts have created unintended negative consequences of their own. Across the fields of advocacy, mental health, and justice, the most pressing problems stem from a failure to provide sufficiently survivor-centered services. Resources currently available to victims tend to be far too inflexible and uniform.

We have proposed three essential principles to guide future efforts to return to an antiessentialist, feminist approach to domestic violence responses: *voice*—responding to the particular contextualized need of individual survivors; *community*—honoring the importance of supportive relationships to victim safety; and *economic empowerment*—prioritizing solutions targeted at battered women for whom poverty creates additional hurdles. We offer this perspective, as well as concrete suggestions for reform, in the hope that they will trigger a rejuvenated critical focus and debate about the future of the battered women's movement.

References

Abel, E. M. (2000). Psychosocial treatments for battered women: A review of empirical research. *Research on Social Work Practice, 10,* 1, 55–77.

Acevedo, M. J. (2000). Battered immigrant Mexican women's perspectives regarding abuse and help-seeking. *Journal of Multicultural Social Work, 8,* 243–282.

Agar, K., & Read, J. (2002). What happens when people disclose sexual or physical abuse to staff at a community mental health centre. *International Journal of Mental Health Nursing, 11,* 70–79.

Ahrens, L. (1980). Battered women's refuges: Feminist cooperatives v. social services institutions. *Radical America, 14,* 41–47.

American Psychiatric Association. (1980). *Diagnostic and statistical manual of mental disorders* (3rd ed.). Washington, DC: Author.

American Psychiatric Association. (1994). *Diagnostic and statistical manual of mental disorders* (4th ed.). Washington, DC: Author.

American Psychological Association. (2003). Guidelines on multicultural education, training, research, practice and organizational change for psychologists. *American Psychologist, 58,* 377–402.

Anderson, D. J. (2003). The impact on subsequent violence of returning to an abusive partner. *Journal of Comparative Family Studies, 34,* 93–112.

Andrews, B., Brewin, C. R., & Rose, S. (2003). Gender, social support, and PTSD in victims of violent crime. *Journal of Traumatic Stress, 16,* 421–427.

Arias, I., & Pape, K. T. (1999). Psychological abuse: Implications for adjustment and commitment to leave violent partners. *Violence and Victims, 14,* 55–67.

Bachman, R., & Saltzman, L. E. (1995). *Violence against women: Estimates from the redesigned national crime victimization survey, special report.* Washington, DC: U.S. Department of Justice, Bureau of Justice Statistics.

Baker, P. L. (1997). And I went back. *Journal of Contemporary Ethnography, 26,* 55–70.

Baker-Miller, J. (1993). Growth through relationships. *Advanced Development, 5,* 13–25.

Baldry, A. C. (2003). Bullying in schools and exposure to domestic violence. *Child Abuse & Neglect, 27,* 713–732.

Ballou, M. (2005). Threats and challenges to feminist therapy. *Women & Therapy, 28*(3–4), 201–210.

Ballou, M., Matsumoto, A., & Wagner, M. (2002). Toward a feminist ecological theory of human nature: Theory building in response to real-world dynamics. In M. Ballou & L. S. Brown (Eds.), *Rethinking mental health and disorder: Feminist perspectives* (pp. 99–141). New York: Guilford Press.

Bardasi, E., & Gornick, J. C. (2003). Women and part-time employment: Workers' "choices" and wage penalties in five industrialized countries. In D. J. Pevalin & D. Rose (Eds.), *A researcher's guide to the National Statistics Socioeconomic Classification* (pp. 209–244). London: Sage.

Barnett, O. W. (2001). Why battered women do not leave, Part 2: External inhibiting factors—Social support and internal inhibiting factors. *Trauma, Violence, & Abuse, 2,* 3–35.

Barnett, O. W., Martinez, T. E., & Keyson, M. (1996). The relationship between violence, social support, and self-blame in battered women. *Journal of Interpersonal Violence, 11,* 221–233.

Bartky, S. L. (1997). Sympathy and solidarity: On a tightrope with Scheler. In D. T. Meyers (Ed.), *Feminists rethink the self: Feminist theory and politics* (pp. 177–196). Boulder, CO: Westview Press.

Bassuk, E. L., Buckner, J. C., Weinreb, L. F., Browne, A., Bassuk, S. S., Dawson, R., & Perloff, J. N. (1997). Homelessness in female-headed families: Childhood and adult risk and protective factors. *American Journal of Public Health, 87,* 241–248.

Bassuk, E. L., Dawson, R., Perloff, J. N., & Weinreb, L. F. (2001). Post-traumatic stress disorder in extremely poor women: Implications for health care clinicians. *Journal of the American Medical Women's Association, 56,* 79–85.

Bassuk, E. L., Melnick, S., & Browne, A. (1998). Responding to the needs of low-income, homeless women who are survivors of family violence. *Journal of the American Medical Women's Association, 53,* 57–64.

Belenky, M., Clinchy, B., Goldberger, N., & Tarule, J. (1986). *Women's ways of knowing.* New York: Basic Books.

Bell, C. C., & Mattis, J. (2000). The importance of cultural competence in ministering to African American victims of domestic violence. *Violence Against Women, 6,* 515–532.

Bell, M., & Goodman, L. A. (2001). Supporting battered women involved with the court system: An evaluation of a law school-based advocacy intervention. *Violence Against Women, 7*, 1377–1404.

Bell, M. E., Goodman, L. A., & Dutton, M. A. (in press). The dynamics of staying and leaving: Implications for battered women's emotional well-being and experiences of violence at the end of a year. *Journal of Family Violence.*

Belle, D. (1983). The impact of poverty on social networks and supports. *Marriage and Family Review, 5*, 89–103.

Bennett, L., Goodman, L. A., & Dutton, M. A. (1999). Systemic obstacles to the criminal prosecution of a battering partner: A victim perspective. *Journal of Interpersonal Violence, 14*, 761–772.

Bennett Cattaneo, L., & Goodman, L. A. (2005). Risk factors for reabuse in intimate partner violence: A cross-disciplinary critical review. *Trauma, Violence, & Abuse, 6*, 141–175.

Bennett Cattaneo, L., & Goodman, L. A. (2007). New Directions in IPV risk assessment: An empowerment approach to risk management. In K. Kendall-Tackett & S. Giacomoni (Eds.), *Intimate partner violence* (pp. 1–17). New York: Civic Research Institute.

Benson, M. L., & Fox, G. L. (2004). *Economic distress, community context, and intimate violence: An application and extension of social disorganization theory.* Washington, DC: National Institute of Justice.

Bent-Goodley, T. B. (2004). Perception of domestic violence: A dialogue with African-American women. *Health & Social Work, 29*, 307–316.

Bograd, M. (1999). Strengthening domestic violence theories: Intersections of race, class, sexual orientation, and gender. *Journal of Marital and Family Therapy, 25*, 275–289.

Bond, L. A., Belenky, M. F., & Weinstock, J. S. (2000). The listening partners program: An initiative toward feminist community psychology in action. *American Journal of Community Psychology, 28*, 697–730.

Bonisteel, M., & Green, L. (2005, June). *Implications of the shrinking space for feminist anti-violence advocacy.* Paper presented at the Canadian Social Welfare Policy Conference, Forging Social Futures, Fredericton, New Brunswick, Canada.

Brabeck, K. (2003). Testimonio: A strategy for collective resistance, cultural survival and building solidarity. *Feminism & Psychology, 13*, 252–258.

Brabeck, M., & Brown, L. (1997). Feminist theory and psychological practice. In J. Worell & N. G. Johnson (Eds.), *Shaping the future of feminist psychology: Education, research, and practice* (pp. 15–35). Washington, DC: American Psychological Association.

Bradley v. State, 1 Miss. (1 Walker) 156 (1824).

Breslau, N., Davis, G. C., Andreski, P., & Peterson, E. (1991). Traumatic events and posttraumatic stress disorder in an urban population of young adults. *Archives of General Psychiatry, 48,* 216–222.

Brief for the National Network to End Domestic Violence as Amici Curiae Supporting Respondents, Davis v. Washington, Hammon v. Indiana, 126 S. Ct. 2266 (2006) (Nos. 05-5224 and 05-5705).

Briere, J., & Jordan, C. E. (2004). Violence against women: Outcome complexity and implications for assessment and treatment. *Journal of Interpersonal Violence, 19,* 1252–1276.

Brown, J. (1997). Working toward freedom from violence: The process of change in battered women. *Violence Against Women, 3,* 5–26.

Brown, L. S. (1990). The meaning of a multicultural perspective for theory-building in feminist therapy. *Women & Therapy, 9,* 1–21.

Brown, L. S. (1994). *Subversive dialogues: Theory in feminist therapy.* New York: Basic Books.

Brown, L. S. (2004). Feminist paradigms of trauma treatment. *Psychotherapy: Theory, Research, Practice, Training, 41,* 461–471.

Brown, L. S. (2005, August). *Still subversive after all these years: The relevance of feminist therapy in an age of evidence-based practice.* Carolyn Wood Sherif Awards Address presented at the 113th Annual Convention of the American Psychological Association, Washington, DC.

Browne, A. (1987). *When battered women kill.* New York: Free Press.

Browne, A., & Bassuk, S. S. (1997). Intimate violence in the lives of homeless and poor housed women: Prevalence and patterns in an ethnically diverse sample. *American Journal of Orthopsychiatry, 67,* 261–278.

Browne, A., Salomon, A., & Bassuk, S. S. (1999). The impact of recent partner violence on poor women's capacity to maintain work. *Violence Against Women, 5,* 393–426.

Brownmiller, S. (1975). *Against our will: Men, women and rape.* New York: Simon & Schuster.

Budde, S., & Schene, P. (2004). Informal social support interventions and their role in violence prevention: An agenda for future evaluation. *Journal of Interpersonal Violence, 19,* 341–355.

Burstow, B. (1992). *Radical feminist therapy: Working in the context of violence.* Newbury Park, CA: Sage.

Burstow, B. (2003). Toward a radical understanding of trauma and trauma work. *Violence Against Women, 9,* 1293–1317.

Butler, S. (1978). *Conspiracy of silence: The trauma of incest.* San Francisco: New Glide Publications.

Butts Stahly, G. (1999). Women with children in violent relationships: The choice of leaving may bring the consequence of custodial challenge. *Journal of Aggression, Maltreatment & Trauma, 2,* 239–251.

Buzawa, E. S., & Buzawa, C. G. (1992). The scientific evidence is not conclusive: Arrest is no panacea. In R. J. Gelles & D. R. Loseke (Eds.), *Current controversies in family violence* (pp. 337–341). Thousand Oaks, CA: Sage.

Bybee, D. I., & Sullivan, C. M. (2002). The process through which a strengths-based intervention resulted in positive change for battered women over time. *American Journal of Community Psychology, 30,* 1, 103–132.

Bybee, D., & Sullivan, C. M. (2005). Predicting re-victimization of battered women 3 years after exiting a shelter program. *American Journal of Community Psychology, 36,* 85–96.

Cachelin, F. M., & Striegel-Moore, R. H. (2006). Help seeking and barriers to treatment in a community sample of Mexican American and European American women with eating disorders. *International Journal of Eating Disorders, 39,* 154–161.

Cahn, D. D. (1992). *Conflict in intimate relationships.* New York: Guilford Press.

Caiazza, A., Shaw, A., & Werschkul, M. (2004). *Women's economic status in the states: Wide disparities by race, ethnicity, and region.* Washington, DC: Institute for Women's Policy Research.

California Institute of Mental Health. (2000). *The CALWorks Project, prevalence report.* Sacramento, CA: Author.

Campbell, J. C. (2002). Health consequences of intimate partner violence. *The Lancet, 359,* 1331–1336.

Campbell, J., Rose, L., Kub, J., & Nedd, D. (1998). Voices of strength and resistance: A contextual and longitudinal analysis of women's responses to battering. *Journal of Interpersonal Violence, 13,* 743–762.

Campbell, J. C., Sharps, P., & Glass, N.E. (2000). Risk assessment for intimate partner violence. In G. F. Pinard & L. Pagani (Eds.), *Clinical assessment of dangerousness: Empirical contributions* (pp. 136–167). New York: Cambridge University Press.

Campbell, J. C., & Soeken, K. L. (1999). Women's responses to battering over time: An analysis of change. *Journal of Interpersonal Violence, 14,* 21–40.

Campbell, J. C., Sullivan, C. M., & Davidson, W. S. (1995). Depression in women who use domestic violence shelters: A longitudinal analysis. *Psychology of Women Quarterly, 19,* 237–255.

Campbell, J. C., Webster, D., Koziol-McLain, J., Block, C., Campbell, D., Curry, M. A., et al. (2003). Risk factors for femicide in abusive relationships: Results from a multisite case control study. *American Journal of Public Health, 93,* 1089–1097.

Capaldi, D. M., Shortt, J. W., & Crosby, L. (2003). Physical and psychological aggression in at-risk young couples: Stability and change in young adulthood. *Merrill–Palmer Quarterly, 49,* 1–27.

Carlson, B. E., McNutt, L.-A., Choi, D. Y., & Rose, I. M. (2002). Intimate partner abuse and mental health: The role of social support and other protective factors. *Violence Against Women, 8,* 720–745.

Chalk, R., & King, P. A. (1998). *Violence in families: Assessing prevention and treatment programs.* Washington, DC: National Academy Press.

Chamallas, M. (1999). *Introduction to feminist legal theory.* New York: Aspen Publishers.

Chamallas, M. (2003). *Introduction to feminist legal theory* (2nd ed.). New York: Aspen Publishers.

Chemtob, C. M., & Carlson, J. G. (2004). Psychological effects of domestic violence on children and their mothers. *International Journal of Stress Management, 11,* 209–226.

Chiu, E. (2001). Confronting the agency in battered mothers. *Southern California Law Review, 74,* 1223–1273.

Clark, A. H., & Foy, D. W. (2000). Trauma exposure and alcohol use in battered women. *Violence Against Women, 6,* 37–48.

Clines, F. X. (2002, January 8). Judge's domestic violence ruling creates an outcry in Kentucky, *New York Times,* p. A114.

Coker, A. L., Davis, K. E., Arias, I., Desai, S., Sanderson, M., Brandt, H. M., & Smith, P. H. (2002). Physical and mental health effects of intimate partner violence for men and women. *American Journal of Preventive Medicine, 23,* 260–268.

Coker, A. L., Smith, P. H., Bethea, L., King, M. R., & McKeown, R. E. (2000). Physical health consequences of physical and psychological intimate partner violence. *Archives of Family Medicine, 9,* 451–457.

Coker, D. (2000). Shifting power for battered women: Law, material resources, and poor women of color. *U.C. Davis Law Review, 33,* 1009–1055.

Coker, D. (2001). Crime control and feminist law reform in domestic violence law: A critical review. *Buffalo Criminal Law Review, 4,* 801–860.

Coker, D. (2004). Race, poverty, and the crime centered response to domestic violence. *Violence Against Women, 10,* 1331–1353.

Coley, S. M., & Beckett, J. O. (1988). Black battered women: Practice issues. *Social Casework, 69,* 483–490.

Colorado Security Deposit Act, Col. Rev. Stat. § 38-12-402 (2006).

Cook, S. L., & Goodman, L. A. (2006). Beyond frequency and severity: Development and validation of the Brief Coercion and Conflict Scales. *Violence Against Women, 12,* 1050–1072.

Correia, A., & VonDeLinde, K. M. (2002). *Integrating anti-poverty work into domestic violence advocacy: Iowa's experience.* Harrisburg, PA: National Resource Center on Domestic Violence, Pennsylvania Coalition on Domestic Violence.

Crenshaw, K. (1991). Mapping the margins: Intersectionality, identity politics, and violence against women of color. *Stanford Law Review, 43,* 1241–1299.

Crenshaw, K. (1992). Race, gender and sexual harassment. *Southern California Law Review, 65,* 1467–1476.

Cumming, E. (1965). Policeman as philosopher, guide, and friend. *Social Problems 12,* 276–281.

Cunradi, C. B., Caetano, R., & Schafer, J. (2002). Socioeconomic predictors of intimate partner violence among White, Black, and Hispanic couples in the United States. *Journal of Family Violence, 17,* 377–389.

Curry, M. A., Perrin, N., & Wall, E. (1998). Effects of abuse on maternal complications and birth weight in adult and adolescent women. *Obstetrics and Gynecology, 92,* 530–534.

Curtis-Fawley, S., & Daly, K. (2005). Gendered violence and restorative justice: The views of victim advocates. *Violence Against Women, 11,* 603–638.

Daly, K., & Stubbs, J. (2006). Feminist engagement with restorative justice. *Theoretical Criminology, 10,* 9–28.

Danis, F. S. (2006). A tribute to Susan Schechter. *Journal of Women and Social Work, 21,* 336–341.

Das Dasgupta, S., & Eng, P. (2003). *Safety & justice for all: Examining the relationship between the women's anti-violence movement and the criminal legal system.* New York: Ms. Foundation for Women. Retrieved May 24, 2007, from http://www.ms.foundation.org/user–ssets/PDF/Program/safety_justice.pdf

Davidson, J. R., Hughes, D., Blazer, D. G., & George, L. K. (1991). Posttraumatic stress disorder in the community: An epidemiological study. *Psychological Medicine, 21,* 713–721.

Davies, J., Lyon, E., & Monti-Catania, D. (1998). *Safety planning with battered women: Complex lives/difficult choices.* Thousand Oaks, CA: Sage.

Davis v. Washington, 126 S. Ct. 2266 (2006).

de Beaumanoir, P. (1992). *Coutumes de Beauvaisis* [Habits of Beauvaisis] (F. R. P. Akehurst, Trans.). Philadelphia: University of Pennsylvania Press. (Original work published c. 1283)

DeJong, C., & Burgess-Proctor, A. (2006). A summary of personal protection order statutes in the United States. *Violence Against Women, 12,* 68–88.

DeLeon-Granados, W., Wells, W., & Binsbacher, R. (2006). Arresting developments: Trends in female arrests for domestic violence and proposed explanations. *Violence Against Women, 12,* 355–371.

District of Columbia Court Reorganization Act of 1970, 84 Stat. 473, Section 131(a) (1970), *codified at* D.C. Code Ann. Section 16–1005(c)(10)(2006).

Dobash, R. E., & Dobash, R. (1979). *Violence against wives.* New York: Free Press.

Donnelly, D. A., Cook, K. J., Van Ausdale, D., & Foley, L. (2005). White privilege, color blindness, and services to battered women. *Violence Against Women, 11,* 6–37.

Donnelly, D. A., Cook, K. J., & Wilson, L. A. (1999). Provision and exclusion: The dual face of services to battered women in three deep south states. *Violence Against Women, 5,* 710–741.

Dugan, L., Nagin, D., & Rosenfeld, R. (2001). *Exposure reduction or backlash? The effects of domestic violence resources on intimate partner homicide: Final report.* Washington, DC: U.S. Department of Justice.

Dunham, K., & Senn, C. Y. (2000). Minimizing negative experiences: Women's disclosure of partner abuse. *Journal of Interpersonal Violence, 15,* 251–261.

Dutton, M. A. (1992). *Empowering and healing the battered woman.* New York: Springer Publishing Company.

Dutton, M. A., & Goodman, L. A. (2005). Coercion in intimate partner violence: Toward a new conceptualization. *Sex Roles, 52*(11/12), 743–756.

Dutton, M. A., Goodman, L. A., & Bennett, L. (1999). Court-involved battered women's responses to violence: The role of psychological, physical, and sexual abuse. *Violence and Victims, 14,* 89–104.

Eby, K. K. (1996). *Experience of abuse and stress: A path model of their joint effects on women's psychological and physical health.* Unpublished doctoral dissertation, Michigan State University.

Economic Stability Working Group of the Transition Subcommittee of the [Massachusetts] Governor's Commission on Domestic Violence. (2002). *Voices of survival: The economic impacts of domestic violence, A blueprint for action.* Boston: Commonwealth of Massachusetts.

Edwards, L. P. (1992). Reducing family violence: The role of the family violence council. *Juvenile and Family Court Journal, 43*(3), 1–18.

Eisenberg, S., & Micklow, P. (1974). *The assaulted wife: "Catch 22" revisited.* Unpublished manuscript.

Epstein, D. (1999). Effective intervention in domestic violence cases: Rethinking the role of prosecutors, judges, and the court system. *Yale Journal of Law & Feminism, 11,* 3–50.

Epstein, D. (2002). Procedural justice: Tempering the state's response to domestic violence. *William and Mary Law Review, 43,* 1843–1905.

Epstein, D., Bell, M. E., & Goodman, L. A. (2003). Transforming aggressive prosecution policies: Prioritizing victims' long-term safety in the prosecution of domestic violence cases. *Journal of Gender, Social Policy & the Law, 11,* 465–498.

Erez, E., & Belknap, J. (1998). In their own words: Battered women's assessment of the criminal processing system's responses. *Violence and Victims, 13,* 251–268.

Erez, E., & Tontodonato, P. (1990). The effect of victim participation in sentencing on sentence outcomes. *Criminology, 28,* 451–474.

Evans, M. E., & Boothroyd, R. A. (2002). A comparison of youth referred to psychiatric emergency services: Police versus other sources. *Journal of the American Academy of Psychiatry and the Law, 30,* 74–80.

Evans, S. (1979). *Personal politics.* New York: Alfred A. Knopf.

Family Violence Prevention Fund. (2007). *Personal stories: Karen.* Retrieved May 29, 2007, from http://www.endabuse.org/programs/display.php3?DocID =100103

The Family Violence Prevention and Services Act, 42 U.S.C. § 10401 et seq. (1984).

Fantuzzo, J. W., & Lindquist, C. (1989). The effects of observing conjugal violence on children: A review and analysis of research methodology. *Journal of Family Violence, 4,* 77–94.

Farmer, A., & Tiefenthaler, J. (2003). Explaining the recent decline in domestic violence. *Contemporary Economic Policy, 21,* 158–172.

Farmer, A., & Tiefenthaler, J. (2004) The employment effects of domestic violence. *Research in Labor Economics, 23,* 301–334.

Ferraro, K., & Pope, L. (1993). Irreconcilable differences: Battered women, police, and the law. In N. Z. Hilton (Ed.), *Local responses to wife assault: Current trends and evaluation*s (pp. 96–123). Newbury Park, CA: Sage.

Finn, M. A. (2003). *Effects of victims' experiences with prosecutors on victim empowerment and re-occurrence of intimate partner violence, final report.* Washington, DC: National Institute of Justice.

Finn, P. (1989). Statutory authority in the use and enforcement of civil protection orders against domestic abuse. *Family Law Quarterly, 23,* 43–73.

Finn, P., & Colson, S. (1990). *Civil protection orders: Legislation, current court practice, and enforcement.* Washington, DC: National Institute of Justice.

Fleury, R. E., Sullivan, C. M., & Bybee, D. I. (2000). When ending the relationship doesn't end the violence: Women's experiences of violence by former partners. *Violence Against Women, 6,* 1363–1383.

Follingstad, D. R., Brennan, A. F., Hause, E. S., Polek, D. S. & Rutledge, L. L. (1991). Factors moderating physical and psychological symptoms of battered women. *Journal of Family Violence, 6,* 81–95.

Ford, D. A., & Regoli, M. J. (1992). The preventive impacts of policies for prosecuting wife batterers. In E. S. Buzawa & C. G. Buzawa (Eds.), *Domestic violence: The changing criminal justice response* (pp. 181–207). Westport, CT: Auburn House.

145

Ford, D., & Regoli, M. (1993). The criminal prosecution of wife assaulters: Processes, problems, and effects. In N. Z. Hilton (Ed.), *Local responses to wife assault: Current trends and evaluations* (pp. 127–164). Newbury Park, CA: Sage.

Freeman, J. (1975). *The politics of women's liberation: A case study of an emerging social movement.* New York: David McKay.

Frieze, I. H. (2005). Female violence against intimate partners: An introduction. *Psychology of Women Quarterly, 29,* 229–237.

Gelles, R. J. (1988). Violence and pregnancy: Are pregnant women at greater risk of abuse? *Journal of Marriage and the Family, 50,* 841–847.

Gergen, M. (2001). *Feminist reconstructions in psychology: Narrative, gender, and performance.* Thousand Oaks, CA: Sage.

Gilligan, C. (1982). *In a different voice: Psychological theory and women's development.* Cambridge, MA: Harvard University Press.

Golding, J. M. (1999). Intimate partner violence as a risk factor for mental disorders: A meta-analysis. *Journal of Family Violence, 14,* 99–132.

Gomez, C., & Yassen, J. (2007). Revolutionizing the clinical frame: Individual and social advocacy practice on behalf of trauma survivors. *Journal of Aggression, Maltreatment & Trauma, 14,* 245–263.

Gondolf, E. W., & Fisher, E. R. (1988). *Battered women as survivors: Alternatives to treating learned helplessness.* Lexington, MA: Lexington Books.

Goodkind, J. R., Gillum, T. L., Bybee, D. I., & Sullivan, C. M. (2003). The impact of family and friends' reaction on the well-being of women with abusive partners. *Violence Against Women, 9,* 347–373.

Goodman, L. A., Bennett, L., & Dutton, M. A. (1999). Obstacles to domestic violence victims' cooperation with the criminal prosecution of their abusers: The role of social support. *Violence and Victims, 14,* 427–444.

Goodman, L. A., Dutton, M. A., Vankos, N., & Weinfurt, W. (2005). Women's resources and use of strategies as risk and protective factors for re-abuse over time. *Violence Against Women, 11,* 311–336.

Goodman, L. A., Dutton, M. A., Weinfurt, K., & Cook, S. (2003). The Intimate Partner Violence Strategies Index: Development and application. *Violence Against Women, 9,* 163–186.

Goodman, L., Fels, K., & Glenn, C. (2006, September). *No safe place: Sexual assault in the lives of homeless women.* Retrieved May 24, 2007, from http://new.vawnet.org/Assoc_Files_VAWnet/AR_SAHomelessness.pdf

Goodman, L. A., Koss, M., & Russo, N. (1993). Violence against women: Mental health effects. Part II: Conceptualizations of posttraumatic stress. *Applied and Preventive Psychology, 2,* 123–130.

Goodmark, L. (1999). From property to personhood: What the legal system should do for children in family violence cases. *West Virginia Law Review, 102,* 237–338.

Goodmark, L. (2003). Law is the answer? Do we know that for sure? *St. Louis University Public Law Review, 23,* 7–48.

Gordon, L. (1988). The frustrations of family violence social work: An historical critique. *Journal of Sociology & Social Welfare, 15,* 139–160.

Graham-Kevan, N., & Archer, J. (2003). Intimate terrorism and common couple violence: A test of Johnson's predictions in four British samples. *Journal of Interpersonal Violence, 18,* 1247–1270.

Grauwiler, P., & Mills, L. G. (2004). Moving beyond the criminal justice paradigm: A radical restorative justice approach to intimate abuse. *Journal of Sociology & Social Welfare, 31,* 46–69.

Green, B., & Sanchez-Hucles, J. (1997). Diversity: Advancing an inclusive feminist psychology. In J. Worell & N. G. Johnson (Eds.), *Shaping the future of feminist psychology: Education, research and practice* (pp. 173–203). Washington DC: American Psychological Association.

Greenfield, L. A., Rand, M. R., Craven, D., Klaus, P. A., Perkins, C. A., Ringel, C., et al. (1998). *Violence by intimates: Bureau of Justice Statistics fact book* (NCJ 167237). Washington, DC: U.S. Department of Justice.

Greenwald, R. (Ed.). (2002). *Trauma and juvenile delinquency: Theory, research, and interventions.* Binghamton, NY: Haworth Press.

Griffing, S., Ragin, D. F., Sage, R. E., Madry, L., Bingham, L. E., & Primm, B. J. (2002). Domestic violence survivors' self-identified reasons for returning to abusive relationships. *Journal of Interpersonal Violence, 17,* 306–319.

Grigsby, N., & Hartman, B. R. (1997). The barriers model: An integrated strategy for intervention with battered women. *Psychotherapy: Theory, Research, Practice, Training, 34,* 485–497.

Gunther, J., & Jennings, M. A. (1999). Sociocultural and institutional violence and their impact on same-gender partner abuse. In J. C. McClennen & J. Gunther (Eds.), *A professional guide to understanding gay and lesbian domestic violence: Understanding practice interventions* (pp. 29–34). Lewiston, NY: Edwin Mellen Press.

Haaken, J., & Yragui, N. (2003). Going underground: Conflicting perspectives on domestic violence shelter practices. *Feminism & Psychology, 13,* 49–71.

Haddad, P., & Knapp, M. (2000). Health professionals' views of services for schizophrenia—Fragmentation and inequality. *Psychiatric Bulletin, 24,* 47–50.

Hamby, S. L. (2000). The importance of community in a feminist analysis of domestic violence among Indians. *American Journal of Community Psychology, 28,* 649–669.

Hamel, J. (2005). *Gender-inclusive treatment of intimate partner abuse: A comprehensive approach.* New York: Springer Publishing Company.

Hanna, C. (1996). No right to choose: Mandated victim participation in domestic violence prosecution. *Harvard Law Review, 109,* 1850–1910.

Hart, B. (1996). Battered women and the criminal justice system. In E. S. Buzawa & C. G. Buzawa (Eds.), *Do arrests and restraining orders work?* (pp. 98–114). Thousand Oaks, CA: Sage.

Hart, S. D., Cooke, D. J., & Michie, C. (2006, March). *The precision of actuarial risk assessment instruments: Evaluating the "margins of error" of group versus individual predictions of violence.* Paper presented at the Annual Meeting of the American Psychology–Law Society, Tampa, FL.

Harvey, M. R. (1996). An ecological view of psychological trauma and trauma recovery. *Journal of Traumatic Stress, 9,* 3–23.

Harway, M., & Hansen, M. (1993). Therapist perceptions of family violence. In M. Hansen & M. Harway (Eds.), *Battering and family therapy: A feminist perspective* (pp. 42–53). Newbury Park, CA: Sage.

Helfrich, C. A., & Simpson, E. (2006). Improving services for lesbian clients: What do domestic violence agencies need to do? *Health Care for Women International, 27,* 344–361.

Helzer, J. E., Robins, L. N., & McEvoy, L. (1987). Post-traumatic stress disorder in the general population: Findings of the Epidemiological Catchment Area survey. *New England Journal of Medicine, 317,* 1630–1634.

Hembree, E., & Foa, E. (2003). Interventions for trauma-related emotional disturbances in adult victims of crime. *Journal of Traumatic Stress, 16,* 187–199.

Hemmens, C., Strom, K., & Schlegel, E. (1998). Gender bias in the courts: A review of the literature. *Sociological Imagination, 35,* 22–42.

Herman, J. L. (1992). *Trauma and recovery.* New York: Basic Books.

Heron, R. L., Twomey, H. B., Jacobs, D. P., & Kaslow, N. J. (1997). Culturally competent interventions for abused and suicidal African American women. *Psychotherapy: Theory, Research, Practice, Training, 34,* 410–424.

Hien, D., & Hien, N. M. (1998). Women, violence with intimates, and substance abuse: Relevant theory, empirical findings, and recommendations for future research. *American Journal of Drug and Alcohol Abuse, 24,* 419–438.

Hill, M., & Ballou, M. (2005). From the past toward the future. *Women & Therapy, 28,* 3–4, 161–163.

Hirschel, D., & Buzawa, E. (2002). Understanding the context of dual arrest with directions for future research. *Violence Against Women, 8,* 1449–1473.

Holden, G. W., Geffner, R. A., & Jouriles, E. N. (Eds.). (2000). *Children exposed to marital violence: Theory, research, and applied issues.* Washington, DC: American Psychological Association.

Holt, V., Kernic, M., Lumley, T., Wolf, M., & Rivara, F. (2002). Civil protection orders and risk of subsequent police-reported violence. *Journal of the American Medical Association, 288,* 589–594.

Holt, V., Kernic, M., Wolf, M., & Rivara, F. (2003). Do protection orders affect the likelihood of future partner violence and injury? *American Journal of Preventive Medicine, 24,* 16–21.

Holzworth-Munroe, A., Meehan, J. C., Herron, K., Rehman, U., & Stuart, G. L. (2000). Testing the Holzworth-Munroe and Stuart (1994) batterer typology. *Journal of Consulting and Clinical Psychology, 68,* 1000–1019.

hooks, b. (1984). *Feminist theory: From margins to center.* Cambridge, MA: South End Press.

Hotaling, G., & Buzawa, E. S. (2003). *Victim satisfaction with criminal justice case processing in a model court setting. Final report to the Department of Justice* (NCJ 195668). Lowell: University of Massachusetts Lowell, Department of Criminal Justice.

Hotaling, G. T., & Sugarman, D. B. (1986). An analysis of risk markers in husband to wife violence: The current state of knowledge. *Violence and Victims, 1,* 101–124.

Hotton, T. (2001). Spousal violence after marital separation. *Juristat, 21,* 1–19.

Housekamp, B. M., & Foy, D. W. (1991). The assessment of posttraumatic stress disorder in battered women. *Journal of Interpersonal Violence, 6,* 367–375.

Hwang, W. (2006). The psychotherapy adaptation and modification framework: Application to Asian Americans. *American Psychologist, 61,* 702–715.

Institute for Children and Poverty. (2002, April). *The hidden migration: Why New York City shelters are overflowing with families.* New York: Author.

Jackson, H., Philp, E., Nuttall, R. L., & Diller, L. (2002). Traumatic brain injury: A hidden consequence for battered women. *Professional Psychology: Research and Practice, 33,* 39–45.

Jackson, S. (1998). Telling stories: Memory, narrative and experience in feminist research and theory. In K. Henwood, C. Griffin, & A. Phoenix (Eds.), *Standpoints and differences: Essays in the practice of feminist psychology* (pp. 45–64). Thousand Oaks, CA: Sage.

Jacobson, N. S., Gottman, J. M., Gortner, E., Berns, S., & Shortt, J. W. (1996). Psychological factors in the longitudinal course of battering: When do the couples split up? When does the abuse decrease? *Violence and Victims, 11,* 371–392.

Johnson, H. (2003). The cessation of assaults on wives. *Journal of Comparative Family Studies, 34,* 75–91.

Johnson, H., & Hotton, T. (2003). Losing control: Homicide risk in estranged and intact intimate relationships. *Homicide Studies, 7,* 58–84.

Johnson, M. P. (1995). Patriarchal terrorism and common couple violence: Two forms of violence against women in U.S. families. *Journal of Marriage and the Family, 57,* 283–294.

Johnson, M. P. (2006). Conflict and control: Gender symmetry and asymmetry in domestic violence. *Violence Against Women, 12,* 1003–1018.

Johnson, M. P., & Ferraro, K. J. (2000). Research on domestic violence in the 1990s: Making distinctions. *Journal of Marriage and the Family, 62,* 948–963.

Johnson, M. P. & Leone, J. M. (2005). The differential effects of intimate terrorism and situational couple violence. *Journal of Family Issues, 26,* 3, 322–349.

Jontz, L. (2006). Note, eighth circuit to battered Kenyan—Take a safari: Battered immigrants face new barrier when reporting domestic violence. *Drake Law Review, 55,* 195–231.

Jordan, J. V. (Ed.). (1997). *Women's growth in diversity: More writings from the Stone Center.* New York: Guilford Press.

Jordan, J. (2001). A relational–cultural model: healing through mutual empathy. *Bulletin of the Menninger Clinic, 65,* 92–103.

Jordan, J. V., & Hartling, L. M. (2002). New developments in relational–cultural theory. In M. Ballou & L. S. Brown (Eds.), *Rethinking mental health and disorder: Feminist perspectives* (pp. 48–70). New York: Guilford Press.

Kane, R. (2000). Police responses to restraining orders in domestic violence incidents: Identifying the custody-threshold thesis. *Criminal Justice and Behavior, 27,* 561–580.

Kanuha, V. K. (1990). Compounding the triple jeopardy: Battering in lesbian of color relationships. In L. Brown & M. P. P. Roots (Eds.), *Diversity and complexity in feminist therapy* (pp. 169–184). Binghamton, NY: Harrington Park/Haworth.

Kaplan, A. (1997). Domestic violence and welfare reform. *Welfare Information Network: Issues Notes, I*(8), 1–9.

Kasturirangan, A., Krishnan, S., & Riger, S. (2004). The Impact of culture and minority status on women's experience of domestic violence. *Trauma, Violence, & Abuse, 5,* 318–332.

Kearney, M. H. (2001). Enduring love: A grounded formal theory of women's experience of domestic violence. *Research in Nursing and Health, 24,* 270–282.

Keilitz, S. L. (1997). *National Center for State Courts, Civil Protection Orders: The benefits and limitations for victims of domestic violence.* Williamsburg, VA: National Center for State Courts.

Kelly, L. (1996). Tensions and possibilities: Enhancing informal responses to domestic violence. In J. L. Edleson & Z. C. Eisikovitz (Eds.), *Sage series on violence against women: Vol. 3. Future interventions with battered women and their families* (pp. 67–86). Thousand Oaks, CA: Sage.

Kelly, V. (1997). Interpersonal violence education of mental health professionals: Survey and curriculum. *Dissertation Abstracts International, 58,* 2683.

Kemp, A., Green, B. L., Hovanitz,, C., & Rawlings, E. I. (1995). Incidence and correlates of posttraumatic stress disorder in battered women: Shelter and community samples. *Journal of Interpersonal Violence, 10,* 43–55.

Kessler, R. C., McGonagle, K. A., Zhao, S., Nelson, C. B., Hughes, M., Eshleman, S., et al. (1994). Lifetime and 12-month prevalence of *DSM–III–R* psychiatric disorders in the United States: Results from the National Comorbidity Survey. *Archives of General Psychiatry, 51,* 8–19.

Kessler, R. C., Sonnega, A., Bromet, E., Hughes, M., & Nelson, C. B. (1995). Posttraumatic stress disorder in the National Comorbidity Survey. *Archives of General Psychiatry, 52,* 1048–1060.

Khamphakdy-Brown, S., Jones, L. N., Nilsson, J. E., Russell, E. B., & Klevens, C. L. (2006). The empowerment program: An application of an outreach program for refugee and immigrant women. *Journal of Mental Health Counseling, 28,* 38–47.

Kilpatrick, D. G., Acierno, R., Resnick, H. S., Saunders, B. E., & Best, C. L. (1997). A 2-year longitudinal analysis of the relationships between violent assault and substance use in women. *Journal of Consulting and Clinical Psychology, 65,* 834–847.

Kim, M. (2002). *Innovative strategies to address domestic violence in Asian and Pacific Islander communities: Emerging themes, models and interventions.* San Francisco: Asian and Pacific Islander Institute on Domestic Violence.

Kimmel, M. S. (2002). Gender symmetry in domestic violence: A substantive and methodological research review. *Violence Against Women, 8,* 1332–1363.

Kitzmann, K. M., Gaylord, N. K., Holt, A. R., & Kenny, E. D. (2003). Child witnesses to domestic violence: A meta-analytic review. *Journal of Consulting and Clinical Psychology, 71,* 339–352.

Klein, A. (2004, October). Dear readers. *National Bulletin on Domestic Violence Prevention, 1–2,* 4–6.

Klein, C. & Orloff, L. (1993). Providing legal protection for battered women: An analysis of state statutes and case law. *Hofstra Law Review, 21,* 801–1189.

Kocot, T., & Goodman, L. A. (2003). The roles of coping and social support in battered women's mental health. *Violence Against Women, 9,* 1–24.

Koss, M., Goodman, L., Browne, A., Fitzgerald, L., Keita, G., & Russo, N. (1994). *No safe haven: Male violence against women at home, at work, and the community.* Washington, DC: American Psychological Association.

Kubany, E. S., Hill, E. E., & Owens, J. A. (2003). Cognitive trauma therapy for battered women with PTSD: Preliminary findings. *Journal of Traumatic Stress, 16,* 81–91.

Kunerth, J. (1997, December 21). She got a job and his abuse. *The Orlando Sentinel*, p. A1.

Lapidus, L. M. (2003). Doubly victimized: Housing discrimination against victims of domestic violence. *Journal of Gender, Social Policy & the Law, 11*, 377–391.

Latta, R. E., & Goodman, L. A. (2005). Gaining access: An assessment of community responsiveness to the needs of Haitian immigrant women who are survivors of intimate partner violence. *Violence Against Women, 11*, 1441–1464.

Lemon, S. C., Verhoek-Oftedahl, W., & Donnelly, E. F. (2002). Preventive healthcare use, smoking, and alcohol use among Rhode Island women experiencing intimate partner violence. *Journal of Women's Health and Gender-Based Medicine, 11*, 555–562.

Lempert, L. B. (1996). Women's strategies for survival: Developing agency in abusive relationships. *Journal of Family Violence, 11*, 269–289.

Levendosky, A., Bogat, G. A., Theran, S. A., Trotter, J. S., von Eye, A., & Davidson, W. S. (2004). The social networks of women experiencing domestic violence. *American Journal of Community Psychology, 34*, 95–109.

Levin, R., McKean, L., & Raphael, J. (2004, January). *Pathways to and from homelessness: Women and children in Chicago shelters*. Center for Impact Research. Retrieved November 20, 2006, from http://www.impactresearch.org/publications

Liang, B., Glenn, C., & Goodman, L. A. (2005). Feminist ethics in advocacy relationships: A relational vs. rule-bound approach. *The Community Psychologist, 38*, 26–28.

Lindhorst, T., & Padgett, J. D. (2005). Disjunctures for women and frontline workers: Implementation of the Family Violence Option. *Social Service Review, 79*, 406–429.

Litwack, T. R. (2001) Actuarial versus clinical assessments of dangerousness. *Psychology, Public Policy, and Law, 7*, 409–443.

Lloyd, S., & Taluc, N. (1999). The effects of male violence on female employment. *Violence Against Women, 5*, 370–392.

Logan, T., Shannon, L., & Walker, R. (2005). Protective orders in rural and urban areas: A multiple perspective study. *Violence Against Women, 11*, 876–911.

Logan, T., Shannon, L., Walker, R., & Faragher, T. M. (2006). Protective orders: Questions and conundrums. *Trauma, Violence, & Abuse, 7*, 175–205.

Loke, T. (1997, Winter). Trapped in domestic violence: The impact of United States immigration laws on battered immigrant women. *Boston University Public Interest Law Journal, 6*, 589–628.

Loseke, D. R. (1992). *The battered woman and shelters: The social construction of wife abuse*. Albany: State University of New York Press.

Lott, B. (2002). Cognitive and behavioral distancing from the poor. *American Psychologist, 57,* 100–110.

Lott, B., & Bullock, H. E. (2007). *Psychology and economic injustice: Personal, professional, and political intersections.* Washington, DC: American Psychological Association.

Lundy, M., & Grossman, S. (2001). Clinical research and practice with battered women: What we know, what we need to know. *Trauma, Violence, & Abuse, 2,* 120–141.

Lyon, E. (1998). *Poverty, welfare, and battered women: What does the research tell us?* (Welfare and Domestic Violence Technical Assistance Initiative). Harrisburg, PA: National Resource Center on Domestic Violence.

Margolin, G. (2005). Children's exposure to violence: Exploring developmental pathways to diverse outcomes. *Journal of Interpersonal Violence, 20,* 72–81.

Martin, A. J., Berenson, K. R., Griffing, S., Sage, R. E., Madry, L., Bingham, L. E., et al. (2000). The process of leaving an abusive relationship: The role of risk assessments and decision-certainty. *Journal of Family Violence, 15,* 109–122.

Martin, D. (1976). *Battered wives.* San Francisco: Glide.

Maxian, M. (2000). Paved with good intentions: Mandatory arrest and decreasing the threshold for assault. *Fordham Urban Law Journal, 27,* 629–671.

Maxwell, C. D., Garner, J. H. & Fagan, J. A. (1999, June). *The impact of arrest on domestic violence: Results from five policy experiments.* Paper presented at the Research in Progress Seminar, Washington, DC.

McClennen, J. C. (2005). Domestic violence between same-gender partners: Recent findings and future research. *Journal of Interpersonal Violence, 20,* 149–154.

McCloskey, L. A., Figueredo, A. J., & Koss, M. P. (1995). The effects of systemic family violence on children's mental health. *Child Development, 66,* 1239–1261.

McCloskey, L. A., & Walker, M. (2000). Posttraumatic stress in children exposed to family violence and single-event trauma. *Journal of the American Academy of Child & Adolescent Psychiatry, 39,* 108–115.

McWilliams, N. (2005). Preserving our humanity as therapists. *Psychotherapy: Theory, Research, Practice, Training, 42,* 139–151.

Meier, J. (1997). Domestic violence, character, and social change in the welfare reform debate. *Law & Policy, 19,* 205–265.

Meier, J. (2003). Domestic violence, child custody, and child protection: Understanding judicial resistance and imagining the solutions. *Journal of Gender, Social Policy & the Law, 11,* 657–725.

Merrill, G. S., & Wolfe, V. A. (2000). Battered gay men: An exploration of abuse, help seeking and why they stay. *Journal of Homosexuality, 39,* 1–30.

Miccio, G. K. (2005). A house divided: Mandatory arrest, domestic violence, and the conservatization of the battered women's movement. *Houston Law Review, 42,* 237–323.

Miethe, T. D. (1987). Stereotypical conceptions and criminal processing: The case of the victim–offender relationship. *Justice Quarterly, 4,* 571–593.

Miller, J. B. (1987). *Toward a new psychology of women* (2nd ed.). Boston: Beacon Press.

Miller, J. B., & Stiver, I. P. (1997). *The healing connection: How women form relationships in therapy and in life.* Boston: Beacon Press.

Mills, L. G. (1998). Mandatory arrest and prosecution policies for domestic violence: A critical literature review and the case for more research to test victim empowerment approaches. *Criminal Justice and Behavior, 25,* 306–318.

Mills, L. G. (1999). Killing her softly: Intimate abuse and the violence of state interventions. *Harvard Law Review, 113,* 550–613.

Miranda, J., Green, B., Krupnick, J., Chung, J., Siddique, J., Belin, T., & Revicki, D. (2006). One-year outcomes of a randomized clinical trial treating depression in low-income minority women. *Journal of Consulting and Clinical Psychology, 74,* 99–111.

Mitchell, K. J., & Finkelhor, D. (2001). Risk of crime victimization among youth exposed to domestic violence. *Journal of Interpersonal Violence, 16,* 944–964.

Moe, A. M., & Bell, M. P. (2004). Abject economics: The effects of battering and violence on women's work and employability. *Violence Against Women, 10,* 29–55.

National Center for Injury Control and Prevention. (2003). *Costs of intimate partner violence against women in the United States.* Atlanta, GA: Centers for Disease Control and Prevention.

National Council of Juvenile and Family Court Judges. (1990). *Family violence: Improving court practice.* Reno, NV: Author.

National Institute of Justice, U.S. Department of Justice. (1990). *National Crime victim survey.* Washington, DC: Author.

National Law Center on Homelessness and Poverty. (2006, March). *Domestic violence and housing: Why was VAWA necessary?* Washington, DC. Author.

National Research Council, Committee on Law and Justice, Division of Behavioral and Social Sciences and Education. (2004). Advancing the Federal Research Agenda on Violence Against Women. In C. Kruttschnitt, B. L. McLaughlin, & C. V. Petrie (Eds.), *Workshop on issues in research on violence against women* (pp. 96–100). Washington, DC: National Academy Press.

Norcross, J. D. (2005). Lose not our moorings: Commentary on McWilliams (2005). *Psychotherapy: Theory, research, practice, training, 42,* 152–155.

NOW Legal Defense and Education Fund. (2002). *The impact of violence in the lives of working women: Creating solutions, creating change.* New York: Author.

Nurius, P. S., Furrey, J., & Berliner, L. (1992). Coping capacity among women with abusive partners. *Violence and Victims, 7,* 229–243.

O'Brien, K. M., & Murdock, N. L. (1993). Shelter workers' perceptions of battered women. *Sex Roles, 29,* 183–194.

O'Brien, M. J. R., John, R. S., Margolin, G., & Erel, O. (1994). Reliability and diagnostic efficacy of parents' reports regarding children's exposure to marital aggression. *Violence and Victims, 9,* 45–62.

O'Faolain, J., & Martines, L. (Eds.). (1979). *Not in god's image: Women in history.* London: Virago. (Original work published 1974)

Office of the U.S. Surgeon General. (1986). *Workshop on violence and public health. U.S. Department of Health and Human Services Report* (Publication No. HRS-D-MC 86-1). Washington, DC: Health Resources and Services Administration, U.S. Public Health Service, U.S. Department of Health and Human Services.

Oliver, W. (2000). Preventing domestic violence in the African American community: The rationale for popular culture interventions. *Violence Against Women, 6,* 533–549.

Omnibus Consolidated Appropriations Act of 1997, 104 Pub. L. 208, § 350 (1996), *codified at* 8 U.S.C. § 1227(a)(2)(E)(2006).

Pagelow, M. (1984). *Family violence.* New York: Praeger.

Parker, B., McFarlane, J., & Soeken, K. (1994). Abuse during pregnancy: Effects on maternal complications and birth weight in adult and teenage women. *Obstetrics and Gynecology, 84,* 323–328.

Peled, E., & Edleson, J. L. (1994). Advocacy for battered women: A national survey. *Journal of Family Violence, 9,* 285–296.

Peled, E., Eisikovitz, Z., Enosh, G., & Winstok, Z. (2000). Choice and empowerment for battered women who stay: Toward a constructivist model. *Social Work, 45,* 9–25.

Pence. E. (2001). Advocacy on behalf of battered women. In C. Renzetti, J. Edelson, & R. Bergen (Eds.), *Sourcebook on VAW* (pp. 329–344). Thousand Oaks, CA: Sage.

Pence, E. L., & Shepard, M. L. (1999). An introduction: Developing a coordinated community response. In M. F. Shepard & E. L. Pence (Eds.), *Coordinating community responses to domestic violence: Lessons from Duluth and beyond* (pp. 3–23). Thousand Oaks, CA: Sage.

Pennell, J. (2005). Widening the circle. In J. Pennell & G. Anderson (Eds.), *Widening the circle: The practice and evaluation of family group conferencing with children, youths, and their families* (pp. 1–8). Washington, DC: NASW Press.

Pennell, J. (2006). Stopping domestic violence or protecting children? Contributions from restorative justice. In D. Sullivan & L. Tifft (Eds.), *Handbook of restorative justice: A global perspective* (pp. 286–298). London: Taylor & Francis.

Pennell, J., & Burford, G. (2000). Family group decision-making and family violence. In G. Burford & J. Hudson (Eds.), *Family group conferences: New directions in community-centered child and family practice* (pp. 171–192). Hawthorne, NY: Aldine de Gruyter.

Pennell, J., & Burford, G. (2002). Feminist praxis, Making family group conferencing work. In H. Strang & J. Braithwaite (Eds.), *Restorative justice and family violence: New ideas and learning from the past* (pp. 108–127). Cambridge, England: Cambridge University Press.

Pennell, J., & Francis, S. (2005). Safety conferencing: Toward a coordinated and inclusive response to safeguarding women and children. *Violence Against Women, 11,* 666–692.

Pleck, E. (1987). *Domestic tyranny: The making of social policy against family violence from colonial times to the present.* New York: Oxford University Press.

The Protection from Discriminatory Eviction for Victims of Domestic Violence Amendment Act, D.C. Code Ann. § 42-3505.01(c-1) (2006).

Ptacek, J. (1999). *Battered women in the courtroom: The power of judicial response.* Boston: Northeastern University Press.

Puzone, C. A. (2000). National trends in intimate partner homicide: United States, 1976–1995. *Violence Against Women, 6,* 409–426.

Pyles, L. (2006). Toward safety for low-income battered women: Promoting economic justice strategies. *Families in Society, 87,* 63–70.

Rand, M. R. (1990). *Crime and the nation's households* (NCJ 130302). Washington, DC: Department of Justice, Bureau of Justice Statistics.

Rand, M. R. (1997). *Violence-related injuries treated in hospital emergency departments.* Washington, DC: U.S. Department of Justice, Bureau of Justice Statistics.

Rap, A., & Silverman, J. (2002). Violence against immigrant women: The roles of culture, context, and legal immigrant status on intimate partner violence. *Violence Against Women, 8,* 367–398.

Raphael, J. (2000). *Saving Bernice: Battered women, welfare, and poverty.* Boston: Northeastern University Press.

Raphael, J. (2001). Domestic violence as a welfare-to-work barrier: Research and theoretical issues. In C. M. Renzetti, J. L. Edleson, & R. K. Bergen (Eds.), *Sourcebook on violence against women* (pp. 443–456). Thousand Oaks, CA: Sage.

Raphael, J. (2003). Battering through the lens of class. *Journal of Gender, Social Policy & the Law, 11,* 367–368.

Raphael, J. (2004). Rethinking criminal justice responses to intimate partner violence. *Violence Against Women, 10,* 1354–1366.

Raphael, J., & Shapiro, D. L. (2002). *Sisters speak out: The lives and needs of prostituted women in Chicago.* Chicago: Center for Impact Research.

Rebovich, D. (1996). Prosecution response to domestic violence. Results of a survey of large jurisdictions. In E. Buzawa & C. Buzawa (Eds.), *Do arrests and restraining orders work?* (pp. 176–191). Thousand Oaks, CA: Sage.

Reinharz, S. (1994). Toward an ethnography of "voice" and "silence." In E. J. Trickett, R. J. Watts, & D. Birman (Eds.), *Human diversity: Perspectives on people in context* (pp. 178–200). San Francisco: Jossey-Bass.

Rennison, C., & Planty, M. (2003). Non-lethal intimate partner violence: Examining race, gender and income patterns. *Violence and Victims, 18,* 433–443.

Rennison, C. M., & Welchans, S. (2000). *Intimate partner violence.* Washington, DC: U.S. Department of Justice.

Renzetti, C. M. (1992). *Violent betrayal: Partner abuse in lesbian relationships.* Thousand Oaks, CA: Sage.

Resick, P. A, & Schnicke, M. K. (1992). Cognitive processing therapy for sexual assault victims. *Journal of Consulting and Clinical Psychology, 60,* 748–756.

Resnick, H. S., Kilpatrick, D. G., Dansky, B. S., Saunders, B. E., & Best, C. L. (1993). Prevalence of civilian trauma and posttraumatic stress disorder in a representative national sample of women. *Journal of Consulting and Clinical Psychology, 61,* 984–991.

Rhode Island Fair Housing Practice Act, R.I. Gen. Laws §§ 34-37-2.4 (2006).

Richie, B. E. (1985). Battered Black women, a challenge for the Black community. *The Black Scholar, 16*(2), 40–44.

Richie, B. E. (2000). A Black feminist reflection on the antiviolence movement. *Signs, 4,* 1133–1137.

Richie, B. E. (2005). Forward. In N. J. Sokoloff & C. Pratt (Eds.), *Domestic violence at the margins: Readings on race, class, gender, and culture* (pp. xv–xiv). New Brunswick, NJ: Rutgers University Press.

Riger, S., Raja, S., & Camacho, J. (2002). The radiating impact of intimate partner violence. *Journal of Interpersonal Violence, 17,* 184–205.

Rodriguez, N. M. (1988). A successful feminist shelter: A case study of the family crisis center in Hawaii. *Journal of Applied Behavioral Science, 12,* 400–423.

Romkens, R. (2006). Protecting prosecution: Exploring the powers of law in an intervention program for domestic violence. *Violence Against Women, 12,* 160–186.

Rose, L. E., Campbell, J., & Kub, J. (2000). The role of social support and family relationships in women's responses to battering. *Health Care for Women International, 21,* 27–39.

Roth, S., Newman, E., Pelcovitz, D., van der Kolk, B., & Mandel, F. S. (1997). Complex PTSD in victims exposed to sexual and physical abuse: Results from the *DSM–IV* field trial for posttraumatic stress disorder. *Journal of Traumatic Stress, 10,* 539–555.

Rothenberg, B. (2003). "We don't have time for social change": Cultural compromise and the battered woman syndrome. *Gender & Society, 17,* 771–787.

Russo, N. F., & Vaz, K. (2001). Addressing diversity in the Decade of Behavior: Focus on women of color. *Psychology of Women Quarterly, 25,* 280–294.

Sachs, H. (1999). Domestic violence as a barrier to women's economic self-sufficiency. *Welfare Information Network, 3*(10). Retrieved May 24, 2007, from http://www.financeproject.org/Publications/domesticviolence.htm

Sackett, L. A., & Saunders, D. G. (1999). The impact of different forms of psychological abuse on battered women. *Violence and Victims, 14,* 105–117.

Safe Havens Interfaith Partnership Against Domestic Violence. (2002). [Report]. Boston, MA: Safe Havens Family Violence Prevention Project.

Saltzman, L. E., Fanslow, J. L., McMahon, P. M., & Shelley, G. A. (1999). *Intimate partner violence surveillance: Uniform definitions and recommended data elements.* Atlanta, GA: Centers for Disease Control and Prevention, National Center for Injury Prevention and Control.

Sands, S. J., Baker, K., & Cahn, N. (1990). *Police response to domestic violence.* Unpublished manuscript.

Sarason, B. R., Sarason, I. G., & Gurung, R. A. R. (2001). Close personal relationships and health outcomes: A key to the role of social support. In B. R. Sarason & S. Duck (Eds.), *Personal relationships: Implications for clinical and community psychology* (pp. 15–41). New York: Wiley.

Schechter, S. (1982). *Women and male violence: The visions and struggles of the battered women's movement.* Boston: South End Press.

Schechter, S. (2000, February). Introduction. In J. Davies (Ed.), *Building comprehensive solutions to domestic violence. Introduction to policy advocacy and analysis: Improving how systems respond to battered women* (pp. 1–3). Harrisburg, PA: National Resource Center on Domestic Violence.

Scheppers, E., van Dongen, E., Dekker, J., Geertzen, J., & Dekker, J. (2006). Potential barriers to the use of health services among ethnic minorities: A review. *Family Practice, An International Journal, 23,* 325–348.

Schneider, E. M. (2000). *Battered women and feminist lawmaking.* New Haven, CT: Yale University Press.

Scott, E. K., London, A. S., & Myers, N. A. (2002). Dangerous dependencies: The intersection of welfare reform and domestic violence. *Gender & Society, 16,* 878–897.

Sharma, A. (2001). Healing the wounds of domestic abuse: Improving the effectiveness of feminist therapeutic interventions with immigrant and racially visible women who have been abused. *Violence Against Women, 7,* 1405–1428.

Shepard, M. F., & Pence, E. L. (Eds.). (1999). *Coordinating community responses to domestic violence: Lessons from Duluth and beyond.* Thousand Oaks, CA: Sage.

Sherman, L. W. (1993). Defiance, deterrence, and irrelevance: A theory of the criminal sanction. *Journal of Research in Crime and Delinquency, 30,* 445–473.

Sherman, L. W., & Berk, R. A. (1984). The specific deterrent effects of arrest for domestic assault. *American Sociological Review, 49,* 261–272.

Shumaker, D. M., & Prinz, R. J. (2000). Children who murder: A review. *Clinical Child and Family Psychology Review, 3,* 97–115.

Simon, S. (2002, January 22). Judges push for abused to follow the law. *LA Times,* p. A12.

Simpson, E., & Helfrich, C. (2005). Lesbian survivors of intimate partner violence: Provider perspectives on barriers to accessing services. *Journal of Gay & Lesbian Social Services, 18,* 39–59.

Sklar, H., Mykyta, L., & Wefald, S. (2001) *Raise the floor: Wages and policies that work for all of us.* New York: Ms. Foundation for Women.

Skolnik, S. (1997, August 18). Confronting domestic violence: D.C.'s once shoddy record much improved. *Legal Times,* p. 17.

Smith, L. (2005). Psychotherapy, classism, and the poor: Conspicuous by their absence. *American Psychologist, 60,* 687–696.

Smyth, K., Goodman, L., & Glenn, C. (2006). The full-frame approach: A new response to marginalized women left behind by specialized services. *American Journal of Orthopsychiatry, 76,* 489–502.

Snell, J. E., Rosenwald, R., & Robey, A. (1964). The wifebeater's wife: A study of family interaction. *Archives of General Psychiatry, 11,* 107–112.

Sokoloff, N., & Dupont, I. (2005a). Domestic violence at the intersections of race, class, and gender: Challenges and contributions to understanding violence against marginalized women in diverse communities. *Violence Against Women, 11,* 38–64.

Sokoloff, N. J., & Dupont, I. (2005b). Domestic violence: Examining the intersections of race, class, and gender: An introduction. In N. Sokoloff & C. Pratt (Eds.), *Domestic violence at the margins* (pp. 1–14). New Brunswick, NJ: Rutgers University Press.

Spaccarelli, S., Sandler, I. N., & Roosa, M. (1994). History of spouse violence against mother: Correlated risks and unique effects in child mental health. *Journal of Family Violence, 9,* 79–98.

Stahly, G. B. (1999).Women with children in violent relationships: The choice of leaving may bring the consequence of custodial challenge. *Journal of Aggression, Maltreatment & Trauma, 2,* 239–251.

Stark, E. (2006). Commentary on Johnson's "Conflict and control: Gender symmetry and asymmetry in domestic violence." *Violence Against Women, 12,* 1019–1025.

State v. Lucas, 770 N.E.2d 114 (Ohio App. 5th Dist. 2002).

State v. Oliver, 70 N.C. 60 (1874).

Stith, S. M., Rosen, K. H., Middleton, K. A., Busch, A. L., Lundeberg, K., & Carlton, R. P. (2000). The intergenerational transmission of spouse abuse: A meta-analysis. *Journal of Marriage and the Family, 62,* 640–654.

Straus, M. A. (2006). Future research on gender symmetry in physical assaults on partners. *Violence Against Women, 12,* 1086–1097.

Straus, M. A., & Gelles R. J. (1990). *Physical violence in American families: Risk factors and adaptations to violence in 8,145 families.* New Brunswick, NJ: Transaction Publishers.

Straus, M. A., Gelles, R. J., & Steinmetz, S. K. (1980). *Behind closed doors: Violence in the American family.* Garden City, NY: Doubleday.

Strube, M. J., & Barbour, L. S. (1984). Factors related to the decision to leave an abusive relationship. *Journal of Marriage and Family, 46,* 837–844.

Stubbs, J. (2002). Domestic violence and women's safety: Feminist challenges to restorative justice. In H. Strang & J. Braithwaite (Eds.), *Restorative justice and family violence* (pp. 42–61). New York: Cambridge University Press.

Stubbs, J. (2004). *Restorative justice, domestic violence and family violence* (Issues Paper No. 9). Sydney, Australia: Australian Domestic and Family Violence Clearinghouse.

Sue, D. W., & Sue, S. (2003). *Counseling the culturally diverse: Theory and practice.* New York: Wiley.

Sue, S., & Lam, A. G. (2002). Cultural and demographic diversity. In J. C. Norcross (Ed.), *Psychotherapy relationships that work: Therapist contributions and responsiveness to patients* (pp. 401–422). New York: Oxford University Press.

Sullivan, C. M., & Bybee, D. I. (1999). Reducing violence using community-based advocacy for women with abusive partners. *Journal of Consulting and Clinical Psychology, 67,* 43–53.

Sutherland, C. A., Sullivan, C. M., & Bybee, D. I. (2001). Effects of intimate partner violence versus poverty on women's health. *Violence Against Women, 7,* 1122–1143.

Tan, C., Basta, J., Sullivan, C. M., & Davidson, W. S. (1995). The role of social support in the lives of women exiting domestic violence shelters: An experimental study. *Journal of Interpersonal Violence, 10,* 437–451.

Thomas, J. E. (1999). "Everything about us is *feminist*": The significance of ideology in organizational change. *Gender & Society, 13,* 101–119.

Thompson, M. P., Kaslow, N. J., & Kingree, J. B. (2002). Risk factors for suicide attempts among African American women experiencing recent intimate partner violence. *Violence and Victims, 17,* 283–295.

Tiefenthaler, J., Farmer, A., & Sambira, A. (2005). Services and intimate partner violence in the United States: A county-level analysis. *Journal of Marriage and Family, 67,* 565–578.

Tjaden, P. (2004). What is violence against women? Defining and measuring the problem: A response to Dean Kilpatrick. *Journal of Interpersonal Violence, 19,* 1244–1251.

Tjaden, P., & Thoennes, N. (2000). *Extent, nature, and consequences of intimate partner violence: Findings from the National Violence Against Women Survey.* Washington, DC: U.S. Department of Justice, Office of Justice Programs, National Institute of Justice.

Tolman, R. M., & Raphael, J. (2000). A review of research on welfare and domestic violence. *Journal of Social Issues, 56,* 655–682.

U.S. Department of Justice. (1984). *Attorney General's Task Force on Family Violence: Final report.* Washington, DC: Author.

U.S. Department of Justice. (2004, July 21). *Attorney General Ashcroft announces $20 million for communities through President Bush's Family Justice Center Initiative* (press release). Retrieved June 19, 2007, from http://www.usdoj.gov/opa/pr/2004/July/04_opa_499.htm

U.S. Department of Labor. (2004, February). *Consumer expenditures in 2002* (Rep. No. 974). Washington, DC: Bureau of Labor Statistics.

van der Kolk, B. A., Roth, S., Pelcovitz, D., Sunday, S., & Spinazzola, J. (2005). Disorders of extreme stress: The empirical foundation of a complex adaptation to trauma. *Journal of Traumatic Stress, 18,* 389–399.

Vest, J. R., Catlin, T. K., Chen, J. J., & Brownson, R. C. (2002). Multistate analysis of factors associated with intimate partner violence. *American Journal of Preventive Medicine, 22,* 156–164.

Victims of Trafficking and Violence Protection Act (VTVPA), 38 U.S.C. § 101 et seq. (2000).

Violence Against Women Act (VAWA), 42 U.S.C. § 13701 et seq. (1994).

Violence Against Women Act of 2005, Pub. L. 109-162, §§ 601, 606, 607; *codified at* 42 U.S.C. §§ 1437d, 1437f (amended 2006).

Violence Against Women and Department of Justice Reauthorization Act, 42 U.S.C. § 13701 et seq. (2005).

Violence Policy Center. (2005). *When men murder women: An analysis of 2003 homicide data.* Retrieved May 22, 2006, from http://www.vpc.org/study ndx.htm

Violence Policy Center. (2006). *American roulette: Murder–suicide in the United States.* Retrieved May 22, 2006, from http://www.vpc.org/latest.htm

Walker, L. E. (1979). *The battered woman.* New York: Harper & Row.

Walker, L. E. (1984). *The battered woman syndrome.* New York: Springer Publishing Company.

Walker, L. E. (1994). *Abused women and survivor therapy.* Washington, DC: American Psychological Association.

Warshaw, C., & Moroney, G. (2002). *Mental health and domestic violence: Collaborative initiatives, service models, and curricula.* Retrieved May 24, 2007, from http://www.dvmhpi.org/Model%20Collab%2011.6.02.pdf

Websdale, N. (2001). *Policing the poor: From slave plantation to public housing.* Boston: Northeastern University Press.

Weissman, M. M., Bruce, M. L., Leaf, P. J., Florio, L. P., & Holzer, C. I. (1991). Affective disorders. In L. N. Robins & D. A. Regier (Eds.), *Psychiatric disorders in America: The Epidemiologic Catchment Area Study* (pp. 53–80). New York: Free Press.

West, C. M. (2005). Domestic violence in ethnically and racially diverse families. In N. J. Sokoloff (Ed.), *Domestic violence at the margins: Readings on race, class, gender, and culture* (pp. 340–349). New Brunswick, NJ: Rutgers University Press.

Wilcox, P. (2000). "Me mother's bank and me nanan's, you know, support!": Women who left domestic violence in England and issues of informal support. *Women's Studies International Forum, 23,* 35–47.

Wilder Research Center. (2003). *Homeless in Minnesota.* Retrieved May 24, 2007, from http://www.wilder.org/reportsummary.0.html?tx_ttnews[tt_news]=536

Wilt, S. A., Illman, S. M., & Brody Field, M. (1995). *Female homicide victims in New York City 1990–1994.* New York: Department of Health Injury Prevention Programs.

Wolfe, D. A., Crooks, C. V., Lee, V., McIntyre-Smith, A., & Jaffe, P. G. (2003). The effects of children's exposure to domestic violence: A meta-analysis and critique. *Clinical Child and Family Practice, 6,* 171–187.

Wolfe, D. A., Wekerle, C., Reitzel, D., & Gough, R. (1995). Strategies to address violence in the lives of high risk youth. In E. Peled, P. G. Jaffe, & J. L. Edleson (Eds.), *Ending the cycle of violence: Community responses to children of battered women* (pp. 255–274). New York: Sage.

Women and Violence: Hearings Before the Committee on the Judiciary on Legislation to Reduce the Growing Problem of Violent Crimes Against Women, Senate, 101st Cong., 131 (statements of Sarah M. Buel and Susan Kelly-Dreiss) (1990).

Wood, G. G., & Roche, S. E. (2001). Representing selves, reconstructing lives: Feminist group work with women survivors of male violence. *Social Work With Groups, 23*(4), 5–23.

Woods, S. J. (2000). Prevalence and patterns of posttraumatic stress disorder in abused and postabused women. *Issues in Mental Health Nursing, 21,* 309–324.

Wooldredge, J., & Thistlethwaite, A. (2002). Reconsidering domestic violence recidivism: Conditioned effects of legal controls by individual and aggregate levels of stake in conformity. *Journal of Quantitative Criminology, 18,* 45–70.

Worrell, J., & Remer, P. (1992). *Feminist perspectives in therapy: An empowerment model for women.* New York: Wiley.

Yoshioka, M. R., & Choi, D. Y. (2005). Culture and interpersonal violence research: Paradigm shift to create a full continuum of domestic violence services. *Journal of Interpersonal Violence, 20,* 513–519.

Young, C. (2003, June 16). In abuse, men are victims too. *Boston Globe,* p. A15.

Zehr, H. (2004). *Critical issues in restorative justice.* Monsey, NY, and Devon, England: Criminal Justice Press and Willan.

Zweig, J. M., & Burt, M. R. (2006). Predicting case outcomes and women's perceptions of the legal system's response to domestic violence and sexual assault: Does interaction between community agencies matter? *Criminal Justice Policy Review, 17,* 202–233.

Zweig, J. M., Burt, M. R., & Van Ness, A. (2003). *The effects on victims of victim service programs funded by the STOP formula grants program.* Washington, DC: Urban Institute.

Author Index

Abel, E. M., 58, 114
Acevedo, M. J., 18
Acierno, R., 56
Agar, K., 67
Ahrens, L., 36
American Psychiatric Association, 19, 55
American Psychological Association, 117
Anderson, D. J., 93, 97, 98
Andreski, P., 19
Andrews, B., 20
Archer, J., 10
Arias, I., 100

Bachman, R., 21, 105
Baker, K., 72
Baker, P. L., 77, 97
Baker-Miller, J., 96
Baldry, A. C., 23
Ballou, M., 2, 59
Barbour, L. S., 98
Bardasi, E., 129
Barnett, O. W., 25, 97
Bartky, S. L., 39, 90, 91
Bassuk, E. L., 21, 107
Bassuk, S. S., 15, 18, 105
Basta, J., 25
Beckett, J. O., 108

Belenky, M. F., 90
Belknap, J., 78, 97
Bell, C. C., 102
Bell, M. E., 25, 76, 98, 119
Bell, M. P., 105
Belle, D., 103
Bennett, L., 18, 75, 100, 102
Bennett Cattaneo, L., 78, 119n1
Benson, M. L., 132
Bent-Goodley, T. B., 114
Berk, R. A., 72
Berliner, L., 100
Berns, S., 97
Best, C. L., 19, 56
Bethea, L., 18
Binsbacher, R., 9
Blazer, D. G., 19
Bograd, M., 91, 102
Bond, L. A., 90
Bonisteel, M., 35, 36, 41, 46, 53, 57, 68, 69, 93, 113
Boothroyd, R. A., 23
Brabeck, K., 91
Brabeck, M., 2, 59
Bradley v. State, 29
Brank, E. M., xiiin1
Brennan, A. F., 19
Breslau, N., 19

Wagner, M., 59
Walker, L. E., 52, 54, 64
Walker, M., 23
Walker, R., 79, 80
Wall, E., 23
Warshaw, C., 50, 51, 59, 67, 68, 70, 115
Websdale, 78
Wefald, S., 132
Weinfurt, K., 54, 100
Weinfurt, W., 25, 99
Weinreb, L. F., 21
Weinstock, J. S., 90
Weissman, M. M., 19
Wekerle, C., 24
Welchans, S., 18, 93, 98
Wells, W., 9
Werschkul, M., 128
West, C. M., 96
Wilcox, P., 100

Wilder Research Center, 107
Wilson, L. A., 46, 102
Wilt, S. A., 24
Winstok, Z., 43, 97, 121
Wolf, M., 80
Wolfe, D. A., 23, 24
Wolfe, V. A., 9, 12
Women and Violence, 23
Wood, G. G., 64
Woods, S. J., 55
Wooldredge, J., 72n1
Worrell, J., 59

Yassen, J., 51, 62, 63, 66, 116, 117
Yoshioka, M. R., 99
Young, C., 9
Yragui, N., 37, 44, 102, 122

Zehr, H., 125
Zweig, J. M., 12, 85, 94

Subject Index

Legislation
  anti–domestic violence, 36–37
  living-wage, 132
  mandatory-arrest, 72–73
Lesbian couples, 8–9, 12, 117
Lesbian relationships, 102
Lesbian women, 46
Levi Strauss & Co., 129
Lindquist, Tyra, 122
Living-wage legislation, 132
Liz Claiborne, Inc., 130
Longer term assistance, 130–133
"Love Is Not Abuse" program, 130
Loving contrition stage (in cycle of
  violence), 53
Low-Income Housing Tax Credit
  program, 107
Loyalty, to community, 101
Lucas, Betty, 81

Male dominance
  in organizations, 35–36
  in society, 2
Male unemployment, 15, 72n1
Managed care system, 67–68, 116, 117
Mandatory arrest policies, 72–73,
  75–76, 78, 92
Marine, Susan, 61, 67–68
Martin, Del, 32
Massachusetts, 129
Measures of success, 68–69, 93, 113,
  116
Meier, Joan, 38, 39
Mental health, and intimate partner
  violence, 18–21
Mental health models, 57–66
  failings of, 58–59
  feminist therapy theory, 59–66
  types of, 58
Mental health system, 49–70
  and battered woman syndrome,
    52–54
  and battered women as survivors,
    54–55

collaboration, absence of, 69
and community, 103
and definitions of success, 68–69
and economic empowerment, 133
evaluation methods in, 116
explanatory theories in, 51–57
future reforms of, 114–117
models of mental health, 57–66
political response vs., 50–51
and PTSD, 55–57
reimbursement criteria, 67–68,
  116
in supportive communities,
  123–124
and survivor-defined perspective,
  93
systemic limitations of current,
  66–69
training, insufficient, 66–67
Minimum wage, 132
Minneapolis Domestic Violence
  Experiment, 72
Minorities, 117
Mississippi Supreme Court, 29
Monitoring systems, 127n3
Ms. Foundation, 104–105
Murder–suicides, 18

National Center for Juvenile and
  Family Court Judges, 83
National Coalition Against Domestic
  Violence (NCADV), 33, 34
National Crime Survey, 73
National Family Violence Survey, 8
National Housing Law Project, 131n7
National Institute of Justice, 75
National Law Center on Homeless-
  ness and Poverty, 131n7
National Violence Against Women
  Survey (NVAWS), 14–15
Native American women, 128n6
NCADV. *See* National Coalition
  Against Domestic Violence
New Zealand, 125

About the Authors

Lisa A. Goodman, PhD, is an associate professor in the Department of Counseling, Developmental, and Educational Psychology at Boston College and coordinator of the Mental Health Counseling MA Program. She is the author of more than 65 articles and book chapters on institutional and community responses to intimate partner violence; the effects of partner violence on marginalized women, including homeless, low-income, and severely mentally ill populations; and innovative community-based mental health practices for vulnerable populations. She has received grants from the National Institute of Justice and the National Institute of Mental Health to pursue research in these areas. Dr. Goodman is cochair of the American Psychological Association's Task Force on Male Violence Against Women and cofounder of the Reach Out About Depression (ROAD) Resource Team, an advocacy project in Cambridge, Massachusetts, for low-income women struggling with depression.

Deborah Epstein, JD, is a professor of law at Georgetown University Law Center, director of the Domestic Violence Clinic, and associate dean for the Clinical Education and Public Interest & Community Service programs. She helped lead an effort to design and implement one of the nation's first specialized domestic violence courts in Washington, DC, and she served as codirector of the court's Domestic Violence Intake Center. Her scholarship analyzes contemporary efforts to reform systemic responses to those in abusive relationships and suggests new ways to improve the legal system. She is chair of the DC Domestic Violence Fatality Review Board and has served on the DC Mayor's Commission on Violence Against Women, the DC Superior Court Domestic Violence Coordinating Council, and the DC Coalition Against Domestic Violence Board of Directors.